Outside

OUTSIDE

Selected Writings

MARGUERITE DURAS

Translated by Arthur Goldhammer

Beacon Press   Boston

Beacon Press
25 Beacon Street
Boston, Massachusetts 02108

Beacon Press books are published under the auspices
of the Unitarian Universalist Association
of Congregations in North America.

Library of Congress Cataloging in Publication Data

Duras, Marguerite.
Outside: selected writings.

Translated from the French.
1. Duras, Marguerite—Translations, English.
I. Title.
PQ2607.U8245A24   1986   844'.912   86-47507
ISBN 0-8070-6310-X

Text design by David Ford

Contents

CONTENTS

Foreword

Journalism without a moral position is impossible. Every journalist is a moralist. It's absolutely unavoidable. A journalist is
someone who looks at the world and the way it works, someone
who takes a close look at things every day and reports what she
sees, someone who represents the world, the event, for others.
She cannot do her work without judging what she sees. It's impossible. In other words, objective reporting is a complete fraud. A
lie. There is no such thing as objective journalism or an objective
journalist. I have rid myself of many prejudices, but surely the
greatest of them was to have believed in the possibility of objec-
tively reporting an event.

To write for a newspaper is to write immediately. No waiting.
The writing is inevitably affected by the impatience of the medium, by the obligation to write quickly, and is somewhat ne-
glected. The idea of neglecting the writing does not displease me.

You see, I used to write articles for the papers every now and
then. From time to time I wrote for the outside world, when the
outside world overwhelmed me, when things *outside,* in the

street, drove me crazy—or else when I had nothing better to do. Which happened.

I wrote newspaper articles, then, for a variety of reasons, first and foremost to get out of my room. In those days I used to work on my books eight hours a day. When I wrote books I never did articles. It was in the in-between periods, the empty stretches of time, that I became caught up in the outside. When I wrote books I think I didn't even read the papers. The news didn't register with me—I didn't understand what was going on. Writing articles meant going outside—like going to the movies.

As for my other reasons, I needed money. All the articles for *Vogue* were written to earn money for food. And then, too, people asked me to write: I promised to do a regular column for *France-Observateur* and so found myself obliged to write to a deadline, just as I must now meet the deadline of *Libération*.

My other reasons: I was compelled to write for the newspapers by the same irresistible force that led me to the French resistance and the Algerian resistance and to protest against the government, the military, the politicians, and the like. *Like you, like anyone*, I felt an overwhelming urge to denounce injustice of all sorts, whether its victim was a single person or an entire nation. And I felt a similarly irresistible curiosity to understand love gone amok, love that has thrown off all prudence and plunged headlong into crime, dishonor, and infamy—especially when society and its foolish courts permitted themselves to judge— what?—the id, nature itself, as if they would judge a storm or a fire. I have in mind, for instance, my first article, "The Algerian's Flowers," which appears first in this collection. I am think- ing, too, of Nadine from Orange; and of Trash and Stick, two poor kids who were guillotined in 1958 at age eighteen; and of my in- terviews with my friend Georges Figon, when he was released after fourteen years in prison; and of Simone Deschamps of Choisy-le-Roi.

Those were articles for which the stimulus came from outside, and which I was happy to write. There were also some articles I wrote for money for *Constellation* under the name of my aunt, Thérèse Legrand, which no one has managed to find. And there were all those novels we wrote during the war, a whole group of young people, in order to buy butter and cigarettes and coffee on the black market. Nobody has found them either. I've forgotten plenty of articles, too. Books, never. Books I don't forget. I've forgotten plenty of my life. Except for my childhood and what adventures I've been able to have outside the bounds of ordinary life. About everyday life I know almost nothing at all anymore. Except my child.

The other articles have to do with events that paralleled my life. They were written for the reasons already mentioned and a few others besides, different each time, just as every new encounter, friend, love affair, or tragedy is different from all the others.

Obviously, the idea of publishing these pieces was not mine. It never would have occurred to me. The responsibility belongs to Jean-Luc Hennig, the editor in charge of the "Illustrations" series at Albin Michel. So I said to myself, Why not? Why so modest all of a sudden? If writers publish only what they're writing now and not what they wrote yesterday, there wouldn't be any writers, and if people paid attention only to what interests them now and not to what interested them yesterday, we'd be stuck with the sterility of the present—another fraud, the present.

One more remark before I quit: I've made plenty of mistakes. I claim the right to make mistakes.

I haven't judged these articles. Yann Andréa did that for me. I let him. It's no longer any of my business.

Marguerite Duras
6 November 1980

A Note on the Organization of the Articles

We tried to settle on a way of arranging the articles in this book. Printing them in chronological order would have had the advantage of being simple and not requiring any explanation. But it would also have been misleading, because the need to write was different at different times. Another possibility was to group all the articles about well-known celebrities together in one section and all the articles about unknowns in another. But that, too, seemed wrong, because once published every subject became a celebrity in the journalistic sense—a name in current events. All subjects are equivalent; the only interest is the writing that reveals them to the reader. We might have tried grouping the pieces by genre: interviews, book reviews, film reviews, prefaces, and so forth. But this is a shopworn solution and not particularly appropriate for the present collection. For these articles, while belonging to the usual journalistic genres, refuse to be confined by them. They slip from one category to another, breaking all the rules—perhaps because they're written by a writer and not a professional journalist.

Still another possibility was to group them according to the "apparent urgency" of the need they were written to meet: the need to eat, the need to comprehend an extreme of passion, the need to respond to some event, the need to meet a regular column deadline, the need to fulfill a contract with a newspaper, and so on. But such needs, however real, cannot by themselves explain why the articles were written. Hence this classification, too, is wrong. Perhaps the very idea of classification is wrong, because writing is either above order or beneath it, whichever you please. In the end, since classification was both impossible and inevitable, it was done by Marguerite Duras, on the theory of the lesser evil.

We are accordingly arranging the articles in five groups, without regard to date of publication and according to what seemed to us their "historical" amplitude, so far as such a choice was possible. We first tried to group the "summer reading" and the "crime stories" and the articles on literature, and then we gave up trying to put anything together with anything else. Now, it may be that the end result of all this turns out to be a classification of the sort I declared a moment ago to be impossible. If so, it's not important.

What is important is the *writing* of Marguerite Duras. Hence the category, the subject, the article do not matter. Here and there a sentence pushes the story off the page, leaving only the text, the words. The words by themselves. What runs through all the articles is the brilliance of the writing, which overwhelms the news, the journalistic fact. When the reading is done the facts disappear, the richness of the writing remains. Marguerite Duras has given us a series of texts on the days of history, the days to which ordinarily no one pays attention. But Marguerite Duras always writes with her attention fully engaged. Any other reason for writing can only be of secondary importance.

Yann Andréa

The Algerian's Flowers

It's Sunday morning, ten o'clock, at the corner of rue Jacob and rue Bonaparte in Saint-Germain-des-Prés, not quite two weeks ago. A young man is walking toward the corner from the direction of the Buci market. He is twenty years old, miserably dressed, behind a pushcart full of flowers. A young Algerian selling flowers—illegally, but then his whole life is illegal. He walks toward the corner of Jacob and Bonaparte, which is less closely watched than the market, and stops there—anxious, of course.

He has reason to be anxious. Not ten minutes have passed—he hasn't had time to sell a single bouquet—when two gentlemen "in plainclothes" move toward him. They come from rue Bonaparte. They're hunting. Noses in the wind, sniffing the fine Sunday air for irregularities the way a bird dog might sniff for quail, they head straight for their quarry.

"Papers?"

The Algerian has no license to sell flowers.

So one of the two gentlemen goes over to the pushcart, slides his clenched fist underneath, and—how strong he is!—overturns

1

the cart, flowers and all, with a single blow. The intersection fills with the flowers of early spring (Algerian spring).

Eisenstein isn't there to record that image of flowers on the ground, stared at by the young Algerian flanked by France's representatives of law and order. Nobody is there. The first passing cars avoid the flowers, instinctively drive around them—nobody can stop them from doing that.

No one is there. But wait, yes, there is someone, a woman, just one woman. "Bravo!" she shouts. "If the cops always went after them like that, we'd soon be rid of that scum. Bravo!"

But another woman arrives from the direction of the market. She looks at the flowers, and at the young criminal who was selling them, and at the jubilant woman, and at the two plainclothesmen. And without saying a word she bends down, picks up some flowers, walks over to the young Algerian, and pays him. After her another woman comes, picks up some flowers, and pays. Fifteen women. All in silence. The plainclothesmen are fit to be tied. But what can they do? The flowers are for sale and nobody can stop people from wanting to buy them.

The scene lasted just under ten minutes. Not a single flower was left on the ground.

After which the plainclothesmen had all the time they wanted to take the young Algerian off to the station house.

France-Observateur, 1957

Report Card: Could Do Better

Dufresne, age seven, baby-cheeked, crew-cut, asks for the third time to go to the bathroom. The teacher refuses. The moment is crucial: Today the class is studying addition with carrying, the high point of the third trimester. Fifty children are in class. The teacher begins.

He starts with some sticks, putting some down, taking some away. Out of fifty kids, thirty understand. We're at the stage of understanding through images, pure and simple.

The teacher continues. He leaves the sticks on the table and moves to the blackboard, that is, to numbers. He tries to move from understanding to mechanics, to abstraction. Of the thirty still with him after the first part of the lecture, ten will follow him the rest of the way.

Dufresne has not looked at the blackboard. He was playing with a marble, a single marble.

"They can do that," says the teacher. "When they're bored they can play with a marble, a single marble, for an hour."

Another child, Tavernier, did look at the blackboard, with his arms crossed and eyes fixed in a stare, but he saw nothing. "He's never with you," says the teacher. "Tavernier is the worst student in the class. His laziness is vast, inward, uncontrollable." Fournier, small and thin, ahead of his class, not very well behaved, has got it all, the sticks and the numbers, and he leaves the classroom panting with pleasure.

"Fournier," says the teacher, "is blessed. It happens more often than you think, and sometimes it carries them all the way through their schooling. Understanding amuses him. It's not that he's more intelligent than Dufresne, but he shines in the classroom."

"Why?"

"When you try to talk about it," says the teacher, "you feel as though you're entering an endless tunnel that gets wider and wider the further in you go. Why this race in which so few make it to the finish line?"

Leaving aside the complexities of child psychology and educational theory, we asked the teacher, outside of class, to tell us something about Dufresne and Fournier (Tavernier being too unusual a case to warrant further comment).

Dufresne's parents are intellectuals, artists. *Slow learners are found much more often among the children of intellectuals and artists than among those of workers and bureaucrats.* (This is not true at the secondary level.)

Dufresne has almost no sense of responsibility. At home they not only fail to cultivate it, they practically encourage its absence. Dufresne lives on his reputation. He is a legendary troublemaker. They still smile over his bad grades. When other children were still counting blocks, he was visiting art museums. His cheeks are plumper, probably, than those of the other children. *He is a seven-year-old baby, and that's the way he wants it.* For fear that he would catch measles at the neighborhood kindergarten, he learned to read from a private teacher or from his mother. The worst trick that anybody could have played on Dufresne was to send him to school. He literally hates school. He has no idea why he needs to go. Because school destroyed the hitherto perfect order of his world. At home he was never bored in the slightest. There were plenty of visitors who taught him all sorts of things about all kinds of subjects. He knows (has always known) the name Picasso. He has seen Picasso's paintings. Perhaps someone asked his opinion of them. He has traveled in different countries. He has listened to music, possibly watched television. Read books and newspapers. In other words, Dufresne has ideas of his own. More than that, he has a kind of culture, almost, which until he went to school he found perfectly satisfactory. His parents were nonchalant, almost reckless: Dufresne's ideas, apparently original, are not his, really, but theirs. His precocity is completely illusory. Of course a judicious thought might "escape" from time to time, and if it does it will be duly recognized and repeated, because Dufresne is always allowed to say whatever is on his mind. But his real ideas have been nipped in the bud by those around him, almost tragically. He seems to have so many, but in fact he has fewer ideas than other children. Fewer than Fournier, who though silent at the dinner table is seething with ideas. Dufresne will have ideas, of course, but in due course—after his real ideas have been beaten down.

The problem, in short, is that Dufresne was never allowed space to grow. What freedom he had was animal freedom; he renounced his freedom of mind. His intelligence has an adult orientation. Adults taught him things, treating him, almost amorously, as if he were one of them, and protecting him as much as possible from the need to make any effort.

Hence the strictness and egalitarianism of the classroom repelled him to the point that when he first went to school he came home every night and cried. What a grind! To deal with it he brings a trifle with him from home, a mere marble. The marble is home, it is mother. A fetish. With this little marble, he says, I will feel less alone in this horrible place.

Fournier is the son of a civil servant. *Among the children of workers and bureaucrats slow learners are far less common than in other groups.*

Fournier has an exemplary sense of responsibility. It would never occur to him not to do his homework, including the optional exercises. Everybody at home has a schedule. The homework period is part of his. When he is sick, his mother comes to the schoolhouse to get his assignments. Even when he had tonsillitis Fournier did his homework and learned his lessons. Fournier has no reputation. When he misbehaves badly enough, he is punished severely. Bad grades are punished even more. His father is no genius, but he knows that life is not easy and he can't afford to waste money or time on his children's upbringing. At age three Fournier played with blocks. He now has three years of school under his belt. School, for him, is like eating or sleeping, one of life's ineluctable realities. He's just a child of seven. Just his chronological age. Probably, without his being aware of it, he's a little bored at home—the routine there lacks the flexibility, the fantasy that Dufresne finds so difficult to leave behind. Fournier is not only made for school, he likes it. If he has ideas, and if he sometimes expresses them out loud, it is not for the sake of his audience but for the sake of his grades. Hence little Fournier is much more lonely than little Dufresne. There is an emptiness around him, which he populates as he can, but populates alone. What comes out of Fournier's mouth is Fournier's. His precociousness is real. Life has given him a solitude just painful enough to force him to seek out the remedy: effort. He is so used to working hard that it has become a habit. The sticks and the tricks of addition are easily absorbed. Understanding amuses him, as does work. This coincidence makes Fournier a happy student. Nothing impedes his happiness: certainly not homesickness, for no one at home has ever worried about his "case." Not hampered by parents who are too intelligent, Fournier, equal in intelligence to Dufresne, will be more intelligent in school.

The strictness, the egalitarian emptiness of the classroom, satisfy Fournier's needs. He is already familiar with the harsh atmosphere of school. He has fun, though he doesn't realize it, with the sticks and the numbers on the blackboard.

"Just from the way they write in elementary school," the teacher says, "you know what kind of background they come from. And everything follows from that."

Of course there are exceptions. But there are not only exceptions. It would be corrupt in a teacher to believe this too soon, but it is extremely difficult not to believe it at all.

Fournier will skip a grade. The teacher will start over for Dufresne, with or without his sticks. He will expect Dufresne to make a real effort, to put down his marble, his little piece of wood, for ten minutes. He will watch him for weeks, perhaps, seduce him until the marble is forgotten, but not in the way his family has seduced him thus far. The teacher will take the opposite tack, attempting to give his pupil a distant glimpse of the *charm* of hard work in order to bring him back to himself.

France-Observateur, 1957

"The Word *Lilas,* Almost As Tall As It Is Wide"

Germaine Roussel, age 52, born in Amiens, employed as a worker
in a metals processing factory near Paris, has lived in Romainville
for eleven years. She can neither read nor write. Raised on welfare, sent to live with foster parents on a farm near the Somme,
then to a life as a factory worker and mother of two children,
whom she must raise alone, she never had the "leisure" to make
up what she had missed. We tried to overcome our timidity in the
presence of Germaine Roussel, hoping to encourage her to describe her world or—as she herself calls it—her infirmity.

Q. Are there words you recognize without knowing how to
read them?

A. Three. The words for the subway stops I use every day,
Lilas and Châtelet, and my maiden name, Roussel.

Q. Could you recognize them if they were mixed up with lots
of other words?

A. Yes, even if there were twenty other words, I think I
would recognize them.

Q. How do you see them, as patterns?

A. Yes, if you like, as patterns. The word *Lilas* is almost as tall as it is wide. It's pretty. The word *Châtelet* is too stretched out, so to me it seems less pretty. It looks very different from the word *Lilas*.

Q. The times you tried to learn how to read, did it seem difficult to you?

A. You can't imagine. It was awful.

Q. Why so awful?

A. I don't know for sure. Perhaps because it's so . . . small. Excuse me, I'm reaching, I can't express myself.

Q. It must be very difficult for you to live in Paris, to get around, no?

A. If you've got a tongue, you can get to Rome.

Q. What do you do?

A. You have to ask a lot, and think. But you know, we find our bearings very quickly, more quickly than other people. We're like blind people, you know: There are certain spots where we know where we are. And then we ask people.

Q. A lot of people?

A. Maybe ten for an errand in Paris. Once I'm out of Romainville I have to ask. I make mistakes about the names of subway lines, so I have to go back and ask again. And then there are the names of the streets, and shops, and numbers.

Q. Numbers?

A. Yes, I don't know how to read them. I know how to count in my head, I can count my pay and my purchases, but I don't know how to read numbers.

Q. You never tell anyone that you don't know how to read?

A. Never. I always say the same thing, that I forgot my glasses.

Q. Are you ever forced to admit that you can't read?

A. Sometimes, yes, for signatures, at the plant or the city hall. But you see, I always blush when I have to admit the truth. If you were in my place you'd understand.

Q. And what about your work?

A. When I'm interviewed I don't let on. I take my chances every time. Usually it works out all right, except when there are time cards to be filled out every night. Otherwise I just pretend.

Q. Everywhere?

A. Everywhere. At work, at the store, I pretend to check

over the figures and the price tags. I'm afraid that somebody will try to rob me or cheat me. I'm always suspicious.

Q. Do you have trouble in your work?

A. No. I'm a good worker. I have to pay closer attention to what I'm doing than other people. I think about what I'm doing and I'm very careful. I manage.

Q. What about shopping?

A. I know the colors of all the brands I use. When I want to change brands, I take a friend to the store with me. Then I remember the colors of the new brand. People like me have good memories.

Q. What do you do for amusement? The movies?

A. No, I don't understand the movies. Things move too fast, and I don't understand the way they talk. And the worst is when the screen fills with writing. People read a letter and afterward they're upset or happy, but I don't know what's going on. I go to the theater.

Q. Why the theater?

A. There's time to listen. The people say whatever they do. There's nothing written. They speak slowly. I understand a little.

Q. What else?

A. I love the country, and spectator sports. I'm no stupider than other people, but when you don't know how to read you're like a child.

Q. When you hear people talking on the radio, for example, does that give you trouble?

A. Yes, it's the same as with the movies. People use words that are in books. If I'm not used to the people talking or the words they use, somebody has to explain to me afterward, using my own words.

Q. Do you ever forget that you don't know how to read?

A. No, I think about it whenever I leave home. It's tiring and it makes me lose time. I'm always thinking, I hope nobody notices. I'm always afraid.

Q. In what way?

A. I couldn't begin to tell you. It seems to me that it ought to be obvious. It's impossible.

France-Observateur, 1957

Bataille, Feydeau, and God

It may be that the finest contemporary novella was published in 1941 by an author whose name, Pierre Angélique,* has remained unknown. Fifty copies were published at the time, another fifty in 1945, today a few more. The title of the novella is *Madame Edwarda*. . . .

Maurice Blanchot
Nouvelle Revue Française, July 1956

Q. Let me begin, perhaps, with the customary question. Can you tell me what you're working on right now?

A. If you like. I'm working on two things. A preface to a new edition of *Le Coupable* and a work on *Nietzsche and Communism*, which will be volume three of *La Part maudite*.

Q. Volume two being *Erotisme*, just published by Editions de Minuit?

A. Yes. *Nietzsche and Communism* will be concerned with the question of sovereignty, or what I call sovereignty. Nietzsche, in my view, can be forgiven for the prefascist errors in his work.

---

* Pierre Angélique is a pseudonym of Georges Bataille.—Trans.

What justifies Nietzsche's attitude is his search for the sovereign value. If one fails to see that, if one fails to distinguish between that search and the search for military values such as one finds in fascist societies, then Nietzsche is incomprehensible. The sovereignty of man is diametrically opposed to military values. Communism, for example, wants to suppress military values and impose the sovereignty of man—of each man—which it regards as inalienable.

Q. But military values also possess a kind of sovereignty, in the eyes of those who possess military might. How do you distinguish between the two kinds of sovereignty?

A. Military values possess a sovereignty that ceases to be authentically sovereign as soon as the aim is to achieve a precise goal. Think of it this way: the sovereign attitude is diametrically opposed to the attitude involved in work. In work we act in order to gain an advantage. A traveling salesman speaks in order to sell his merchandise. But if we have a sovereign attitude we are indifferent to consequences: we no longer worry about anything. Now, the soldier, the general, aims to achieve a political advantage, and in this he resembles the traveling salesman. Hitler and Louis XIV were also like the traveling salesman in this respect. Nietzsche, on the other hand, defined himself in terms of his refusal to calculate political advantages. For him, something in human life had the sense of a sovereign goal and could not be subordinated to anything else.

The Uniform and Servility

Q. But sovereigns in history have always embodied the military value.

A. Yes. I would raise only one objection to your statement. Originally and fundamentally, sovereignty must have been distinct from military power. Military power might allow itself to assume sovereignty, but the two were distinct. Many traces of that initial state of affairs remain. Ultimately, however, strength won out and swept everything else before it, so that ultimately sovereigns donned uniforms as if bound to demonstrate their servility.

Q. In your view, then, sovereignty cannot have any external

appearance. But isn't there an external appearance that corresponds to sovereignty?

A. Why not? That of a cow in a pasture will do quite nicely, I think.

Q. Is it your view, then, that the sovereignty of man that Nietzsche was seeking is the same as that sought by communism?

A. Communism appears to me necessarily in accord with the sovereignty of human life. For communism there cannot exist any principle that raises itself above human life. It is necessary, however, to show that there is a certain road to communism which, against the wishes of those who choose that road, results in subordinating the individual to something that transcends and alienates him. I don't think that my views in this regard would shock any unbiased Communist.

Q. What subordination do you mean?

A. Often it becomes necessary to place the emphasis on production, on the effort necessary to satisfy needs. In such circumstances it is possible to transcend or alienate the individual in favor of what he is not, if only by limiting the satisfaction of his needs. Man is restricted as the necessary efforts are made. I must discuss this in greater detail, but I am the first to admit that I understand the difficulties that led the Communists at times to take shocking positions.

Q. Where does true sovereignty lead, in your opinion?

A. I think that it leads to privation rather than to privilege. Nietzsche himself at times envisioned a world become socialist in which workers would have had more rights and greater means than intellectuals.

Q. In a transitional period during which access to sovereignty would be easier for intellectuals than for manual laborers?

A. Yes. Ultimately one can envision this as the last difference between the manual laborer and the intellectual.

Q. Can one say that sovereignty, in Nietzsche's view and in yours, is both an open road and a dead end?

A. One can say that the only thing possible in sovereignty is that the image one forms of a man worthy of the name cannot be limited.

Q. How do we achieve such sovereignty, though?

A. No sooner does one move toward it than one encounters God. But it is not possible to reckon with God, whose existence is above one's own. God is nevertheless a concrete indication of the work that one must do within oneself. To place oneself in the position of God is painful: being God is equivalent to being tortured. For being God means that one is in harmony with all that is, including the worst. Being God means having willed the worst. The existence of the worst evils is unimaginable unless God willed them. That, obviously, is a pleasant idea. And a comical one. One cannot think seriously about God without being struck by comic feelings so deep that one can be forgiven for failing to notice that they were comical.

Q. You're laughing?

A. Yes. My idea of God's presence is not only joyful but, if you like, rather similiar to a Feydeau farce. Can you think of a play of Feydeau's that I might use as an example?

Q. I'm thinking . . . nothing comes to mind. And you?

A. No, I can't think of anything either. But I generally forgo imagining concrete things. And in any case I can laugh at God without requiring that he play tricks on me like Feydeau's characters.

The Madman and the Sovereign

Q. What is the major obstacle to the search for sovereignty?

A. No doubt the need to accept the existence of others and to respect that existence fully. On the whole this need yields feelings of profound satisfaction. Except one can never go against a fit of temper. Obviously a temper must never become theoretical. An individual in the grip of his temper is a madman. One might even say that a madman is the perfect image of the sovereign. But a man who could understand that the sovereignty of a sovereign is madness would see all the reasons why he should not behave as a madman.

Q. But you can't banish moods altogether.

A. Of course not. If man should not behave like a madman, still he must give madness its due, as the theater and literature traditionally have done. Again, a temper must never become theoretical. It must never be aimed, for example, against equality.

Q. Shall I go on asking you questions at random?

A. If you like. Let's go on playing ninepins for the pleasure of seeing the pins fall every which way. Go on.

Q. When you are writing—

A. The greatest difficulty for me is not to write at random. What I mean is, it's hard for me to set myself a path while writing.

Q. Until you discover that in fact what you wrote was not at all random?

A. No. Until I *cannot do anything but* make a book.

Q. Is the fact that you have founded a journal of eroticism [*Genèse*, first published in 1958]—a magazine completely divorced from topical concerns—a consequence of your despair with the current political situation?

A. Not at all. I started the journal because, given the radical changes that have taken place in sexual morality in the last few years, such a magazine makes sense.

Q. But you see my point, don't you?

A. Yes. I am not a man who lives in hope. I have never understood how anyone could kill himself for lack of hope. One can be desperate and never for a moment think of killing oneself. Hope is not the only satisfaction.

Q. What else is there?

A. Understanding. I have never been actively involved in politics. What has always mattered to me was to understand. But I had no personal desire. I found the world disgusting. But I've never found a way out of this disgusting world.

Q. I thought that at the time of the Popular Front you glimpsed a way out of this disgusting world.

A. For a very short time it is true that I experienced a political ferment. But before long such questions again began to pass me by. In order to be Communist I would need to be able to invest hope in the world. I lack the vocation of those who feel responsible for the world. Politically, to a certain degree I claim the irresponsibility of the mad. I am not so crazy, but I take no responsibility for the world in any sense whatsoever.

". . . I Am Not Even Communist"

Q. Can I still write that for you communism meets the common need?

A. Yes. I believe that the demands of the workers are at bottom unanswerable by their adversaries. But to repeat, I am not even Communist.

Q. Not even?

A. Since I have no hope in this world and since I live in the present, I cannot concern myself with what will begin only later.

Q. You refuse to concern yourself with it in the stead of others?

A. That's it. Once again, I feel no vocation.

Q. I beg your pardon but I must ask you to say, if you will, whether in the absence of any personal desire or vocation as you call it, you have a wish of a general order.

A. I think that communism is in the order of things, that it is desirable. But the banal expression of my thought distorts this wish somewhat. How about this: I think more or less what other people think. The words *more or less*, coming from someone who tries to express his thought with precision, may be considered essential.

France-Observateur, 1957

On Georges Bataille

Bataille's name alone is enough to intimidate critics. Lacking a ca-
suistry thought to be necessary for dealing with his obscurities, *
critics await a state of grace before undertaking the job. The
years pass, and people continue to entertain the illusion that
some day they will be able to talk about Bataille. Because of this
illusion they never really come to grips with his work, which is of
capital importance. They pride themselves on their abstinence.
They die without having dared confront the bull, out of bound-
less concern for their reputations.

An earnest wish: may the younger generation do it for us, do
what we did not dare to do, without waiting for the one of us who
will dare—to compete with youth.

To say that clarity matters less to Bataille than what kills, than
what murders the habitual concern with clarity that presides
over literary activity in general is to say very little. His work
gives error—broadly understood—its greatest chance. For centuries *Edwarda* will remain sufficiently unintelligible to serve as

the framework of a whole theology. Georges Bataille delivered Edwarda from obscurity but was unable to show any more of her than he shows us: the language at his disposal couldn't fully illuminate her. Because the subject of Edwarda is prior to the usual meanings of language, or beyond them, how can language convey that subject?

One can therefore say of Georges Bataille that he does not write at all, since he writes against language. He is inventing a way of not writing even as he writes. He teaches us to unlearn our literature. The absence of *style* in *Bleu du ciel* is ravishing. It is as if the author had no literary memory behind him. Criticism has nothing firm to grasp. How is it possible to carry nonwriting so far? The word despairs of discharging its function, it loses its inherent magic, it ceases to carry anything but its possible meaning. You feel that at first you got it wrong, only to rediscover its true meaning later on, emancipated, healed of the effects of the bad company it once kept.

It should also be said, perhaps, that the common currency of intelligence is also missing from Bataille's books. Intelligence by itself doesn't make it, but only intelligence in conjunction with physical qualities, with the unknowns of body and mind, like inevitable wounds.

When Edwarda first appears in one of the greatest works of contemporary literature, her tongue is sticking out and she is naked. And when her elder sister Dirty stands out against the *Bleu du ciel* (blue of the sky), she is drunk and squeezes her thighs together while chewing on a filthy curtain.

Edwarda and Dirty are God. Bataille tells us so.

(Nothing could possibly be more obscure but at the same time more clear than this crucial identification. The statement calls for no criticism, in any sense. Criticism either rejects it or allows itself to be swept away, with abandon, into the obscurities of the text. In other words, criticism divorces itself.)

Genet's abjection, so severely criticized by Bataille, expresses the singularity of his characters. It brings them out into themselves, into a royalty that is utterly unique because irreplaceable and "incommunicable." By contrast, Edwarda and Dirty are possessed by dispossession. If Dirty still likes and prefers one person in the world, Edwarda likes and prefers no one. Her prostitution has penetrated her heart. Bataille's abjection, unlike that of Genet, delivers his characters from their singularity and brings them out into their indeterminacy. They are no longer caught in the gangue of an individual royalty but are on their way toward dissolution, toward annihilation: we meet them in passing. That is how Dirty and Edwarda are. Bataille met them one night. They were so little in possession of themselves that their *fate* was no longer in question. Whereas in Genet, the fate of Armand, assumed unto death, moves us deeply. The difference is that between the anonymity of the creature deprived of destiny and the hero who presides over destiny to the point of becoming his own fate.

La Ciguë, 1958

What, They Don't Use the Guillotine Anymore?

(Conversation overheard in a cafe at the Palais-Royal)

"You mean to tell me you haven't figured out that in France they don't use the guillotine anymore?" intones the general.

The general's army is considerably curtailed this evening, consisting of a captain, the captain's wife, and the general's wife, all seated around a cafe table.

"General, I'm sorry to say you're quite right," says the captain. "I scan the papers every morning. Crimes, yes, plenty of crimes, but a death sentence: never."

"France," the general resumes, "has become a country where no one is ever executed. That, my friend, is what has become of France."

The general is of swarthy complexion, revered by his audience. Abd el-Krim was his enemy. His listeners are at attention.

"Shameful," sighs the general.

"Doubt, ah! The benefit of the doubt," the general carries on. "Don't make me laugh. If only it were so simple. When in doubt, that's all the more reason, there's only one thing to do, only one thing: the guillotine. To set an example, you see. I assure you that those fellows would think twice before they tried anything."

"Every night," hazards the captain, "those poor taxi drivers drop like flies."

"And you know," observes the general, "the worst of it is they're not even allowed to carry guns."

"General, it's true," says the captain, "but they say that some of them carry clubs under the seat."

"Good men!" The general's wife remembers the fallen.

"When you come to think of it," says the captain's wife, after much deep thought, "what is there to stop anyone from committing murder? What?"

"In France these days people will commit murder for a thousand francs. Outrageous!" says the general's wife.

"And who pays?" the general suddenly shouts. "Who pays for the months in prison and the food they eat? Who?"

The general, suddenly gripped by democratic fervor, stands in solidarity with the nation.

"We do," says the general. "We, the taxpayer."

The general marshals his rhetoric as he once marshaled his battalions.

"Listen. I know a civilian. He lives near my property in the Hérault. Five years ago this fellow killed his wife. The reason doesn't matter. A clear-cut crime, you'd think, an open-and-shut case. But it's been dragging on for five years, the man's been sitting around waiting to be guillotined! I should add, and this is my point, that this fellow has a piece of property that must be worth— I know what I'm talking about—with the franc where it is today, roughly a million and a half in round numbers. And what if that land were sold to pay for the cost of his imprisonment? Out of the question! We're the ones who have to pay, we, the taxpayers!"

"When you think about it it's unimaginable," the captain's wife sighs. "We're defenseless. On all sides!"

The general takes encouragement from the admiring assent of his audience.

"And self-defense," he screams suddenly, "what about legitimate self-defense?"

An uproar in the cafe. Had the general been attacked? False alarm. The general had not been attacked. Not at all.

"What could be more vague? Nowadays I doubt you even have the right to kill somebody who breaks into your house!"

"It's true," the captain confirms, "that you can be sent to prison for shooting, I repeat, for shooting at an individual who enters your house through, say, a window. Incredible! Incredible!"

The general looks visibly younger. For a brief moment.

"I'm telling you, my legitimate self-defense is my service revolver. They can say what they want. The first man who enters my house without ringing—Ready! Aim! Fire! Bang, bang, bang, bang, bang!"

France-Observateur, 1957

Paris Rabble

Lucie Blin, age 71.

Has just appeared for the fortieth time before the Tribunal of the Seine.

The charge: Theft (shoplifting).

This fortieth time it was two one-piece undergarments from the Louvre Department Store (underwear is what's easiest there). With the goods returned the job only got her four months.

Age 71, then. A widow for thirty years.

Eleven children, seven of them living.

Cannot read or write.

Occupation: Sells flowers illegally. It runs in the family. Her father and mother sold flowers before her. Still, illegally or not, seven children raised. Not one on welfare. So well brought up that they don't want to see her any more. "I understand them," she says.

Banned from Paris for twenty years because of repeated thefts, she never left the city for a single day. Anywhere else she would be lost.

Unfortunately there are times of the year when there are no flowers to sell. For want of flowers Lucie Blin turns to robbery. "I have no choice," she says, "it's impossible." So she steals. Then she goes to court as other people go visiting. They ask her to confess. She confesses, without shame or cynicism: a simple fact, I steal. For the twenty-fifth or the fortieth time she waits until it's over, saying not a word too much in her defense, not polite but not insulting either, and without gratitude for the lawyer who defends her free of charge (the novelist Madeleine Alleins).

"Let me do it my way, I know the scene," she says, refusing one's offer to help, refusing any compromise with honest folk, striking the best bargain with the court just as she does with life.

"I don't want to die yet," she says, "so I must steal."

She has no time to waste. Age 71. She must work quickly. And calculate. She calculates. Yes, she knows the scene. Paris is her jungle. She knows it the way a gutter cat knows the roofs by night. She scurries about, knows her way around. Four months here, six months there—she sails her boat against the wind. She eats. And lives.

"Work, I'm used to it. In prison or out, it doesn't make a whole lot of difference. You wash the floors in the Central Prison or you sell flowers at Les Halles at five in the morning."

She will do it again because she doesn't want to die. Impossible to do anything else. And she will eat. And for the fortieth time "they" won't have her apartment. "Look," she says, "I'm not going to screw my friends. That's the main thing."

France-Observateur, 1957

Tourists in Paris

Since January Paris alone has been host to 700,102 foreign tourists, 220,013 in the first three months of the year, 480,089 in the second three months. *July is not included in these figures.* Last year, in the month of August alone, the number of visitors was 218,603!

Paris is overflowing. By five in the afternoon the cashiers at the Eiffel Tower are haggard with fatigue. They're issuing tickets at the rate of 9,000 per day! At the Louvre the rate is 5,000 tickets per day, 10,000 on Sundays, and at the Musée Grévin it's 4,000.

Twenty-one thousand postcards of the Eiffel Tower arrive every day in New York, Helsinki, Munich, Florence, and other cities of the world. The *Mona Lisa* and the *Coronation of Napoleon I* are not far behind. Followed by "the nudes," not further specified— all nudes, nudes in general, followed by postcards of the *Nike of Samothrace* and the avenue de l'Opéra.

A visit to Paris is regularly concluded with the purchase of a bottle of cognac. Cognac of every brand and label emigrates from France, including brands unknown to the French.

"We're out of Hennessy, but take some Bertrand, you won't re-gret it."

The Bertrand will be carefully carried home to Uncle Ludwig, who won't be any the wiser.

But not all tourists are dupes. There are exceptions to the rule, of course, but those exceptions themselves have rules.

"It's wonderful," says Gisela O., a ravishing young woman of twenty-five, from Hamburg. "It's the first time in my life that so many men have turned to look at me."

"Now you be sure that you go into the stores," says a Roman milliner to a friend of hers about to leave for Paris. "You go in all the stores, ask all the prices, and be sure you don't buy anything. That will be our little revenge."

For what?

We know them all. We're all a little bit guilty. Nobody in the world is less astonished by foreigners than we are. Impassive, Paris has rubbed shoulders with foreigners ever since there has been a tourist trade. We let them discover the city on their own, in the ritually painful manner. For nowhere is one more alone than in Paris—young women from Hamburg apart—and yet more surrounded by crowds. Nowhere is one more likely to incur greater ridicule. And no visit is more essential.

"You've got to get past the first few days," one young American woman tells us. "I spent all my savings to cross the Atlantic, and the first three days I spent crying in my room."

After the first three days—tragic for some, especially the iso-lated intellectuals who disdain to board a bus and join a group tour—the reconciliation takes place. In general this reconcilia-tion is eternal.

Paris Advances Alone Toward Its Destiny

"We'll never make it!" sigh the Americans in the place de la Concorde.

The freedom of Paris is taken for granted. No matter where they come from, they all agree: Even Rome is provincial com-pared with Paris. Here people's free ways jump at the eye. Couples of different colors kiss in the cafes. A man from Senegal walks down the avenue de l'Opéra with his arm around a young blond woman. No mistake is possible: This is Paris.

And, they say, all you have to do is talk to the people of Paris to discover that they govern themselves, that they pay no attention to their bogus government and are sufficiently adult to make up their own minds. Their attitude toward official policy is one of constant mockery. In other words, Paris advances alone toward its destiny; where the people lead no government can follow. Parisian freedom of judgment is exemplary, and so is Parisian distaste for power. Paris reads between the lines of history. It has a good nose. For a hundred and fifty years it has been past deceiving. So much is immediately apparent to everyone.

The freedom of Paris stands revealed in the most unexpected details. Sometimes it comes close to impudence.

"This Gallery of Mirrors that they talk so much about," one Italian says, "if only you knew how dirty the mirrors are! But dirty or not dirty you know perfectly well that people will keep going there, so . . ."

"And the cats," says one Dutch woman, "the cats you have all over the place, that are stretched out everywhere, in their homes and in the tobacconists' shops and in the pharmacies where no one disturbs them, where they sleep right on the drug displays! To us it seems extraordinary!"

"You're Still Driving Cars from the 1930s"

Paradoxically, the freedom of Paris is associated with a persistent belief that nothing in Paris ever changes. Paris, they say, is the city that changes least. After an absence of twenty or thirty years, one still recognizes it.

"Every tourist," says one Spaniard, "begins by looking for Paris 1900: the Paris of the boulevards, of the French Cancan, of *La Belle Hélène*, of Mayol [the music-hall performer—Trans.]. It's expensive at times, but you can't avoid it."

He adds that on the night of his arrival, after hastening to a kiosk to buy *Paris Hollywood*, he naturally headed for Pigalle. And once there he managed to buy a dozen admirably displayed postcards, but only the first one turned out to be anything an-

other than a "madonna from the Louvre." The remaining eleven
cards in the pack were the *Venus de Milo, Mona Lisa,* and so on.
For which he paid 3,000 [old] francs. Quite a sum, when you consider that a room (with female occupant) in the rue Blanche costs
up to 16,000 francs per night and a half hour at a special private
film screening costs 12,000.

Two days later you recover from the shock and discover that
other things remain the same in Paris. One American mentioned
the Citroën 11. "Twenty years ago it astonished Europe, but
there it is, still hanging on! Everywhere else people are driving
new cars, but here you're still driving cars from the 1930s! The
only real change I find after ten years is that the streetwalkers at
La Madeleine have stopped wearing those silver fox stoles that
sustained the erotic dreams of young men around the world."

A word, inevitable, about the flirtatiousness of Frenchmen.
Watch out for them! is the watchword of every female visitor.

"Your reputation is such," says one German, "that if any Frenchman stops at an inn, even if he's missing an arm and sixty years
old, we lock up any girl over the age of sixteen."

We hear that Italian girls can withstand the onslaught, that
Swedish girls rarely dodge, that the Germans don't come any
more until they're grown up and then with chaperones, that the
first time, at least, the Spanish girls are upset at attracting so little
attention, that the English girls ignore whatever attention they
get, and that the Americans never go home again. We might as
well admit that the pleasure of a little danger is not an insignificant part of the charm of Paris for the tourist.

Another word about that charm: Paris is the easiest city in Europe to get around. On that point, too, everyone agrees.

"If only because of the Eiffel Tower, which you can see from
anywhere in the city. Not to mention the Seine, where most of
the avenues begin. And then there's the Metro, whose maps are
so good that you really have to work at it to get lost."

It's expensive, they all say, frightfully expensive, but when they
leave they all talk about coming back some day. We have the defects of our qualities. And they're so used to our defects that if we
made ourselves perfect they would be disoriented and upset.

What we need to do, though, is to make sure they don't encounter the fake Paris. I mean bourgeois Paris, frightfully chau-

vinistic, on its guard as though it were wartime: in other words, the imbeciles.

I remember that a week after some very dear Italian friends came to stay with me, a retired colonel living in the building wrote to my landlord to protest the illegal and disagreeable presence of "foreigners."

I've heard lots of similar stories.

"Imagine," one woman in the hotel trade told me, "I have English clients who reserve a year in advance in order to be sure of seeing Paris. And the Italians, sometimes six months in advance."

Let's make sure they don't run into our imbeciles.

France-Observateur, 1957

The Blue Blood of La Villette*

Along with funerals, this is the ideal sort of place for confirming the saying, "Truth is stranger than fiction."

Opposite the gates of the slaughterhouses, a sign sets the tone:

THE FUTURE, INC.
WHOLESALE OFFAL

On the square the cafes are called Le Bélier d'Argent (The Silver Ram), Le Mouton Blanc (The White Sheep), Le Cochon de Lait (The Milk-Fed Pig), La Comète des Abattoirs (The Comet of the Slaughterhouses), Le Veau d'Or (The Golden Calf), La Tête de Boeuf (The Ox Head), Le Petit Trou de La Villette (The Little Hole of La Villette).

In one cafe a painting depicts a sow sitting next to a piglet in a cradle. The sow is knitting from a pile of tripe.

---

*La Villette is a section of Paris that has long been famous for its stockyards and slaughterhouses.—Trans.

From the entryway the cries of pigs having their throats slit can be heard. Across the way stands a factory that manufactures knives and poleaxes, with a sign that says "We make tenderizers."

We laugh. And then the S.P.C.A. that slumbers within each of us awakens, and we feel pity. Then pity degenerates into literature.

"No steer or hog brought to a public slaughterhouse shall leave the premises except in the form of dead meat," proclaims the general ordinance of 27 June 1914, Chapter 1, Article II. It has the Stendhalian incisiveness of another, better-known article of the Civil Code. Ever since La Villette first came into existence on 1 January 1867, it has had many Jean Genets for whom the poleax has the same erotic glint as the guillotine.

Is this the age of vampires? The slaughtermen, it is known, drink the blood of the beast as it pours from the carotid; the aristocratic lady-friends of the count of Orgel come to drink blood from bowls alongside the slaughtermen, in the scalding rooms.

Is this an age of libertinage? Aragon's French Woman prowls at the gates looking for lovers, making La Villette a magnet for perverts.

La Villette pays no heed. La Villette doesn't care what people say. It slaughters. And every day of the year it unloads upon the eight million residents of greater Paris 770,000 pounds of beef.

Ascetic Slaughtermen

Over toward the Paris-Villette railway station, which smells like manure, like the country, is the livestock market, where five thousand head of cattle are sold on Mondays and two to three thousand head on Thursdays.

On the Paris side of town, which smells of blood and hunger, stand the retail butchers' trucks, waiting.

La Villette works quickly. A steer can be killed, gutted, skinned, and dressed in half an hour by three people.

That is the standard rate. At La Villette as in the Renault plant, the rhythms are hellish, and slaughterhouse workers don't have time for breathers. So you find few cafes, no whorehouse, and no hotel near the slaughterhouses. The count of Orgel's ladies must arrange their assignations for the rue des Saints-Pères or Passy. You find few alcoholics among La Villette workers. The rule is strict: drunks are not allowed. Slaughterman, gut-dresser, or skinner, the day (eight hours, from six in the morning until two in the afternoon) is spent standing in blood—and blood is slippery—knife in hand, face to face with the sometimes skittish animals. The work is dangerous. The good white wine of La Villette is therefore reserved for the tourists and for the songs about Paris, and occasionally for the wholesale butchers who never lay a hand on the meat.

In La Villette at dawn it's Carné; afterward, of course, it's Franju. From midnight until five in the morning the trucks pour in from Normandy, Charolais, Limousin, staying just long enough to unload thousands of hogs, calves, heifers, and steers. Whole herds come pouring out of the railway station. From five until six in the morning, along the Ourcq canal an army of fancy cars pushes back the gates of night.

Behind the wheels of these cars are the big names in meat, the wholesale butchers of Paris. In the livestock market, as big as the place de la Concorde and abutting the slaughterhouses, which themselves cover fifty-two acres, the animals are auctioned off: steer from the Vendée, Limousin, and Charolais from December to June, and the better Norman beef from June to December, along with hogs from the Perigord and sheep from the Causses.

The vocabulary is of course horrifying. The scalding room is where the animals are "iced." Once iced, they are given a "hearse." In La Villette Jacques Prévert would find his fill. In the scalding rooms the man in charge is the wholesale butcher.

He is the boss. The scalding rooms are owned by the city of Paris and offered to the butchers by lot in proportion to their daily sales, as free concessions. There are not many wholesale butchers. There are applicants who applied for licenses fifteen or twenty years ago who have still not received them, and there has been no drawing since 1955, for La Villette has its blue blood, its dynasties. A glance at the membership list of the butchers' association is enough to convince one of this: Lépicier, Jean; Lépicier, Georges; Lépicier, Marcel; Lépicier, Robert (there is also a Monsieur Veau, Mr. Veal). Each wholesale butcher has one or more scalding rooms, but there are also some common rooms available for use by retail butchers and Muslim and Jewish slaughtermen, the latter under the supervision of an official representative of the Jewish community.

The team consists of a head butcher and six journeymen ranked by seniority. The head butcher earns 20,000 francs per week "in beef," 17,000 in veal, and 18,000 in mutton (excluding various bonuses). The number two man earns 17,000 in beef, 13,000 in both veal and mutton. The number three man earns 15,000 in beef, 10,000 in veal, and so on. Head butchers and their assistants all know how to slaughter an animal and on occasion actually do so. All that it takes is the right form, the strength, and the age: one must be at least seventeen. The slaughtermen has his choice of a poleax, club, or revolver, which the regulation states must be "equipped with a single-action hammer."

The regulations are strict. The animals must be taken from the stockyards to the slaughterhouse "at a trot," with whips, without the help of "clubs or biting dogs," "in groups of 25 head of cattle or 300 head of sheep." As a final privilege of innocence, calves "shall be loaded in wagons, standing, without leading strings."

One rule is not observed. It states that animals must be hobbled before being slaughtered. This is to avoid accidents. But it takes two to five minutes to hobble a steer. Here, again, production norms take precedence. To keep up the pace, the precaution is overlooked, increasing the slaughterman's risks fourfold. With a leading string the animal is brought in. Its head is raised. It stretches out its muzzle. The poleax is brought down. The animal falls, dumbstruck. A reed five feet long is inserted in the opening left by the hollow tube (ten inches long) of the poleax, to "kill" the animal's nerves. Such are the stations in La Villette's assembly line, the bolts that have to be turned by these Charlie Chaplins with long knives and blood-stained aprons.

The work generates a lot of blood, an enormous amount of blood: five thousand gallons a day flow over the pavement of La Villette, collected in the central drainage channel of the scalding room. The "blood collectors," "gland collectors," and other ancillary trades of the slaughtering profession supply the drug laboratories on the outskirts of La Villette: Gubler, Rebhun, CPISPA, and others. The rest is used for fertilizer. But beefsteak is La Villette's essential product.

La Villette today is primarily concerned with two problems. The first is beefsteak.

In 1945–46, with the end of rationing, all of France was starved for meat, and for meat of a certain kind. Beefsteak was the symbol of unrationed choice.

Stew reminded people of the Germans, boiled dinner reminded them of the slogans of Marshal Pétain, ribs reminded them of starving cattle. But beefsteak was Gaullist. In a few months the demand for beefsteak rose to three times what it had been before the war. It has risen steadily ever since, and for ten years La Villette has been working hard to find a way to convert one hundred percent of every steer into steak.

The Reign of Beefsteak

The wholesale and retail butchers have almost succeeded. Thanks to clever meat cutting and the advent of "chopped steak," two-thirds of the steer now goes for steak. The remaining third constitutes a problem. During the summer a lot of stew goes to the zoo or the circus. In all seasons there is something left over. How can you force the French housewife to waste an hour of every day making stews and other dishes that require a lot of cooking? To persuade the masses to go back to the good old beef stew of the 1930s would probably take massive advertising, on the scale of Coca Cola. La Villette would need a PR agent. It doesn't have one.

Besides beefsteak, La Villette has another worry, still more serious: if the trend that began ten years ago worsens, La Villette could be in trouble.

"The sales we do now in a year, we used to do in a single season," says one veal broker.

He's right. Although the population of Paris and its suburbs continues to grow steadily, fewer animals pass through La Villette every year. In 1938, 279,392 cattle were slaughtered, compared with 270,016 in 1955 and only 260,585 in 1956. (In 1942, 236,925 animals were slaughtered, 156,380 of which went to the German Reichstelle.)

There are various reasons for this decline. France's cattle herds were never fully replenished after the war. Meat is subject to price controls throughout France, but the prefects who set the prices in the provinces have shown themselves more generous to the butchers than have the authorities in Paris. Since prices are higher in the provinces, particularly for veal, veal has all but deserted La Villette to flood the markets of Marseilles, Lyons, and Bordeaux. Yet the causes of the trend that is threatening La Villette lie still deeper and are more far-reaching than this business of price setting.

Over the past century and a half the French market for meat has twice been profoundly restructured. In prerevolutionary France the slaughtering of livestock was dispersed throughout the country; the free market prevailed. But Napoleon's empire, with its centralizing tendencies, inaugurated a system of municipal slaughterhouses. Five were established in Paris in the time of Napoleon I.

Throughout the nineteenth century the tendency toward greater concentration continued. In 1867 Napoleon III closed the five slaughterhouses in Paris and replaced them with La Villette.

For a half century hence, any meat bound for Paris had to pass through La Villette. But the government maintained tight control over this meat. After World War I, the meat packing trusts attempted to put an end to this state control.

The first to succeed were the wholesale pork butchers. Today, few hogs pass through the scalding rooms of La Villette. Géo, a vertical trust, has its own abattoirs. At Aubervilliers, a company known as La Nationale owns an American-made assembly line that can handle 2,300 hogs per hour at the rate of one hog electrocuted and skinned every forty seconds.

Since World War II the cattle market has evolved in a similar way. More and more, Paris is eating meat slaughtered in the provinces and transported in refrigerated trucks and railway cars. Before long one of the meat trusts will no doubt be in a position to distribute cut beefsteak wrapped in cellophane as in the United States, delivering the meat directly to the retail butcher until it is able to develop its own retail outlets, just as Boussac has opened its chain of "discount stores."

When that happens, La Villette will be a memory. Then the blood of these animals will be spilled in secret. But you can bet that, heading up one of the trusts that will have killed off La Villette, you'll find a Monsieur Veau and two or three Lépiciers.

France-Observateur, 1957

The Duke of Morny's Marshes

Deauville, 15 August. The height of summer. There's a forty-five-mile-an-hour wind. The thermometer is stuck in the mid-fifties—"in the shade," as people say here. Yet Deauville is full.

The streets are almost empty. In the afternoon the nurses and maids show up, because they're paid to. Through the curtains of blowing sand they push prams from Bar de la Mer to Bar du Soleil and back again. No one swims in the raging sea. For a week the umbrellas have been folded. But Deauville is filled to bursting. Not a room to be had for ten miles around. The big hotels opened this year earlier than last. By Easter they were fully booked.

But at night, braving the squalls and the showers, three thousand people came to applaud the Compagnons de la Chanson, singers with the ballet of the Marquis de Cuevas. For August is Deauville's month, the month that leaves people satisfied for the rest of the year. Regardless of the weather. Here the weather is a mere detail. One transcends the weather or else one gets the hell out: there's no happy medium.

If Monsieur André is leaning on the balcony rail surveying his casino on this night of 15 August, he is probably saying what Monsieur Congnac says to himself when he surveys his department store, La Samaritaine: "From the odor alone I can tell how much business I'm doing." The odor of the women of Deauville. As young and beautiful as they are, here they brush against balding men in their fifties, men of superannuated elegance in their white tuxedoes, their faces reduced to uniformity by too many years spent in business or boredom. No unspoiled shopgirl would envy these women their men. Let us hope that they reserve for themselves other pleasures in other seasons, that they take their own vacations.

In any case, these women, like the fifty thousand minor millionaires who "populate" Deauville in season so that they can say afterward that they were there, do not count as far as the casino and its manager Monsieur André are concerned.

Without a maharaja Deauville is deserted.

That Egypt business scared the daylights out of Deauville. The town held its breath.

Three thousand clients can't make up for the one special customer who without batting an eyelash can afford to drop forty-five million francs at baccarat in one night in the Private Room. No matter whether he is king of coffee, of laundry soap, or of several million backward subjects, as long as he can afford to lose with grace. But as national liberation proceeds apace, the management of the casino will be obliged to mix and match, to go after the one big kill. You're either of your time or you're not. And the duke of Windsor, who it seems can't afford to lose more than a million a night, will, in view of his background, play chemin de fer with the king of canned sardines, in view of his income.

The casino has three rooms. One, Le Deauvillais, requires only a suit and tie. L'Union requires evening clothes. And the Private Room—-the Private Room is where Deauville's heart beats. There only gentlemen are admitted. Crowds swarm around them but only to allow them to remain incognito. Incognito is dialectically double: from whom would one hide if one had no reason to hide? What would the celebrities be if they did not stand out against the obscure masses of their fans?

It's raining, it's pouring. In Trouville people eat french fries and shrimp in cafes sheltered from the wind, or they play belote [a card game similar to pinochle—Trans.]. The children yawn with boredom. Between two downpours they will go over to Deauville in order to see "them," so as not to have come all this way for nothing. Last year the casino made a profit of six hundred million, so let's have a look, if only from the outside. And then, forget the storm, let's drive past the Normandie, the Royal, and the Golf—real palaces, those places, only a few like them in the world. And the room rates are not listed: some pay a lot, some pay nothing. There you find the swells hanging around waiting for polo to begin, or for the casino to open, or for the skeet shoot to start, or for a round of golf (all those amusements are owned by the casino). Since the swells come from all over the world, just thinking about them is a way of traveling. Tourists with cars will drive out to the airport at Saint-Gatien to watch Rolls–Royces unloaded from the airplane. The next night Trouville will go back to its simple dreams, its own celebrations, its quick solutions, noisy to be sure but followed by an eternal silence.

No, the truth is there's only one consolation in this city, and that's to go and see the yearlings at the Etablissements Cheri. Since the races at Deauville both compete with and sustain the casino, it was only natural for the casino to take over the track to make sure it would be soundly managed. Hence the Etablissements Cheri also belong to the casino. They were sold a month ago. Lacking anything else to talk about, the city has been talking about this transaction ever since. But the yearlings, given their stage of evolution, remain indifferent. There are three hundred of them, waiting to be sent next month to stud farms around the world. Leaving aside their social fate, they are indeed horses. Their still-frightened eyes do not deceive. They come straight from their mothers and are still ill trained. Their coats gleam, like meadows. You can touch them, and it's true, they're horses, whatever your hands and eyes may say.

France-Observateur, 1957

Country Dancing in Paris

One day, Madame Garnier, a second-hand dealer at 3 rue Saint-Benoît, posted a notice that she was selling out. Widowed and worn out, she was selling her store—one of those things that happens. So there was a property up for sale, but in the rue Saint-Benoît. You can take it for gospel. The news spread like wildfire. Within forty-eight hours all the natives of Rouergue* living in Paris were alerted. And then the parade began.

It went on for a year. Madame Garnier, seated in front of her shop, greeted the folks from Espalion [a town in Rouergue]. Yes, it did indeed go on for a year. "Because," said Madame Garnier, "I want a good seven million for my little store. Seven, I said. Forget five, five and a half, six. I said seven," Madame Garnier persisted, "not a penny less." The neighborhood squinted at her. Some people felt she was asking too much. Would she get it or not? The folks from Espalion paraded past in any case. "I'm in no

* Rouergue is a rugged, remote, and very beautiful section of southern France; its capital is Rodez in Aveyron. Many Paris cafes are owned by natives of this province. —Trans.

3 9

hurry," said Madame Garnier. She had come to Saint-Germain-des-Prés by chance, but she had a good eye. Like everybody else she knew that the coal man had sold what is now the Café Montana for one million instead of the ten it was worth. So she held out, uncompromising. For a year. The folks from Espalion passed up the opportunity for fear of driving up their prices. But Madame Garnier sold just the same, and for seven million, to other buyers. Such things happen.

She won. The neighborhood was happy for her.

But Rouergue does not lose heart. Alert to the least sign of weakness, its armies come and lay siege. They already own all of the Champs-Elysées (except the Derby) and all of the grand boulevards. And this rue Saint-Benoît, five hundred yards long, is the stuff that dreams are made of, as far as the folks from Rouergue are concerned. It's only natural. On this street it's the other way around: nobody is surprised when people sell, only when they don't sell. Still, it's not so simple, even for somebody from Espalion, as the case of Madame Garnier proves. The Armenian hairdresser has been there for twenty years. His place is highly sought after. But what can you do, he loves setting hair! And his neighbor, the old Lithuanian shoemaker, who stubbornly persists in an endless old age, finds a life of patching soles for schoolchildren pleasant enough. What can you do? Of course there is the old ladies' home, a whole building with just twenty-five old women ranging in age from seventy to ninety-one, but they've gotten used to falling asleep to the sounds of the cha-cha-cha when spring arrives and the cellars open their air vents. In another neighborhood they'd be bored.

Rouergue will wait, then. We're holding out. There are our cellars, of course, which the folks from Rouergue have thoroughly explored, but the lower part of the street is no good, the cellars flood the minute the Seine overflows its banks. And the Rivière Bookshop—yes, very likely. But then why not the National Press? Why not the headquarters of the Antialcoholic League on the Boulevard Saint-Germain—irony of fate, the ideal place?

For those who may not know, the town of Espalion counted 3,650 residents at the last census. Compared with 8,100 cafes in Paris. I should mention that in Espalion there's not a single decent cafe. Espalion, a hardworking town, is sober; it has better things to do. Its residents were water-carriers in eighteenth-century Paris. Nowadays—what can I say? The "suburbs" of Espalion are considerable: capital of the country cottage. "This one belongs to the owner of Le Colisée," someone explains, "and this one to the owner of the Royal Concorde, and this one to the owner of the Flore" [all these are fashionable Paris cafes—Trans.].

We have nothing against the folks from Espalion. On the contrary (except perhaps for the neon lighting that makes all their cafes look the same and all their customers seem uniformly pale). But if one tries to "transcend" Rouergue, to achieve a vision at once vivid and objective, a certain comparison cries out to be made, although many people who in all innocence patronize the cafes owned by the folks from Espalion are most likely not in the habit of making it.

France-Observateur, 1957

One out of a Hundred Novels
Makes It to Publication

We asked the editorial director of a major publisher to tell us a little about a literary genre which by its very nature is unknown to the general public, what I call "virtual literature."

Published literature represents only one percent of what is written in the world. It seems worthwhile to talk about the rest, an abyss, a black night out of which comes that "bizarre thing," literature, and into which almost all of it disappears again without a trace.

A moving, sometimes comic, but always poignant tragedy. The editorial director was most kind to grant us an interview. For the past twelve years he has been reading manuscripts at the rate of one a day. For obvious reasons he has asked to remain anonymous.

Q. What lessons can be drawn from years of reading a significant proportion of French literary output?

A. The first thing is that everybody writes. The need to write is in no way related to a particular social status or cultural level. People of all classes write. Farmhands, office workers, factory workers, generals, admirals—everybody.

Q. Is there any geographical pattern to the submissions?

A. No, they're very evenly distributed. People everywhere write. There's at least one would-be writer in every town. In a city of 80,000 you've got to figure there are four or five. Take Orléans, for example. Four or five writers, not counting out-lying farms. When a reader travels in France, he knows that in such-and-such a city at such-and-such an address lives a gentle-man whom he knows very well though they've never met.

Q. What percentage of submissions make it to publication?

A. About one percent. Ninety-nine manuscripts out of a hun-dred are returned to their authors for good.

Q. Can you give a rough classification of this enormous mass of rejects?

A. Yes. First of all there's what I call raw literature. It ac-counts for a third of the manuscripts. You have a lot of retired people in this category, especially people retired from careers in the colonies, as well as military officers and government offi-cials. Their common defect is this: they all think "what a novel my life has been," and they can't distinguish between what is of general interest and what is of interest merely to their own families. They don't succeed in making their writing interesting to the general public. Many of them write in order to correct what they regard as common misconceptions.

Next you have a subcategory, the reformist philosophers. There are a lot of them, raving autodidacts. They invent highly coherent systems, polish them for years, and then try to sell them as remedies for all our ills, recipes for a good government, a sound currency, and a morally healthy society.

Q. The criterion must be hard to establish in this category. How do you distinguish, for example, between one of your phi-losophers and, say, the early Fourier, with his phalanxes?

A. Well, for one thing, none of my philosophers takes any ac-count of reality. And for another thing, they're clearly unedu-cated, although philosophically inclined. They know nothing at all about their predecessors. The more absurd the system, the more vehement the writing and the more convinced the writer is of his own genius. These must be people in a constant rage, to the point that one worries about their neighbors. Especially the ones who live in the country. Sometimes I think I ought to warn the sheriff to keep an eye on some of these people.

Q. Do the writers of raw literature have any notion of how things are done in publishing?

A. Rarely. A few years ago a fellow came to sell me a manuscript. He wanted to make a little money, he said, because he was leaving "the boss lady." He was counting on this manuscript he had in his suitcase and was determined to sell it to me right then and there, on the spot. As far as he was concerned the reading could come later.

Q. What novelists would you include in this group?

A. The ones who create a literature of instinct, along with those who plagiarize and imitate. Of the instinctive writers quite a few write autobiographical novels, especially older women who like to tell their life stories. Their inspiration is a matter of settling scores, punishing evildoers, and righting wrongs.

Q. Any chance of publication?

A. None, or at any rate very little. Nor are the imitative writers likely to find a publisher. You get a lot of folk tales, with plenty of sentimentality and dramatic twists of plot, and you get a lot of people who write like Delly or Paul de Kock. Then you also have the people who plagiarize mystery novels or film plots. They don't stand a chance either.

Q. Would you describe this material as literature?

A. Not really. This stuff is midway between raw literature and what you can really call literature. But raw literature serves a purpose that published literature does not: it unveils its author to an extraordinary degree, lays him bare. In reading these manuscripts we sometimes come upon wonderful scenes, usually episodes from the author's life—scenes of extraordinary fullness and pacing. I remember one prodigious sex scene four or five pages long in a manuscript by a virtual illiterate—a woman.

Q. Why not publish an anthology of such excerpts? Every manuscript reader must have some that he regrets passing up.

A. Because the writers would probably misunderstand the significance of publication.

Q. What, in your opinion, distinguishes the manuscripts with real literary quality?

A. Intelligence. The amplitude of the story. The subordination of particular cases to style. At that point an author writes what he is rather than what he knows.

Q. The subcategories are the same as before, I suppose?

A. Yes, but reinforced, and with talent. You find a compensatory literature but with other models. The models change with time, moreover. Some are enduring.

Q. Could you say a little more?

A. Among the enduring subjects is *Le Grand Meaulnes* [a novel of childhood by Alain-Fournier—Trans.]. It's done a lot of harm. It has spawned a whole literature of childhood fantasy, of out-and-out poetry. This is a decidedly provincial and academic subcategory. There are new models: the Kafkaesque novel, which used to pour in in outrageous numbers but is already on the wane. For the past few years there have been quantities of novels in the manner of Françoise Sagan, which tell of free youth—Bohemian, desperate, bitter. There are enough of those to last five years, but the genre is already falling out of fashion. There is also the American mode (1945–50), which imitates earlier, published imitators.

Q. There must be a true urban literature?

A. Yes, inspired by the models I've just mentioned, leaving aside Alain-Fournier. It describes the boredom of the cities, the solitude of the individual in the urban setting, or rebellion, or the urban adventure.

Q. Is there a literature of Toulouse or of Strasbourg?

A. You know, writers are a breed that negates social and regional differences. Broadly speaking, you would say on the basis of the literary evidence that the majority of the French population is rural. Having said that, however, yes, one might add that certain cities produce books with a specific tone of their own.

Q. Lyons?

A. Intimate novels with a mystical background.

Q. Bordeaux?

A. Social novels. A lot of crumbling ancestral homes. But as long as we're on the subject, why not talk about Swiss novels or Belgian novels?

Q. Swiss novels?

A. Beautifully typed on very fine paper. Noble subject, nebulous, refined. The lakes always play a part, if only as background. Belgian novels are less carefully done.

Q. The French novel belongs to what tradition, still speaking broadly?

A. To the social tradition of Balzac, especially in its provincial aspect. I forgot to mention that one of the most common sources of inspiration is the revolt against the previous generation.

Q. Do you get many North African novels?

A. More and more. The proportion of writers in North Africa is even higher than in France. In France writers avoid topical political subjects, but novels by North African and black writers inevitably have a political dimension.

Q. What is the common trait of all literature, good and bad?

A. The fact that writing is a fierce need, a tragic need, in all writers, often more so in bad writers than in good ones. It is an undertaking that in some cases requires extraordinary moral courage. The writer sacrifices not only leisure time but also work time in order to write his novel. He is always alone, especially if he lives in the provinces, in which case he writes in order to avoid asphyxiation. Needless to say, rejection is always devastating, sometimes tragic. To reject a manuscript, especially a first manuscript, is to reject a whole man, to impugn his being.

Q. What about the miraculous one percent?

A. Yes. Sometimes you recognize it at once. Sometimes it takes several pages, but that's unusual.

Q. How do you recognize it?

A. You immediately feel that you're dealing with a different quality of goods. You feel an immense joy; you tremble. You can't imagine what it will turn out to be. You read on in fear that the quality will fall off, will suddenly disappear. When you reach the end you feel pride, stupid pride, that you discovered the book by chance rather than on someone's recommendation. You tell everybody what you've found.

Q. Do you read every book all the way through?

A. Yes, you can say that I read every one all the way to the end. There's no error of commission. No recommendation sways my opinion, and there's no conspiracy. We're forced by the nature of the publishing business to be conscientious.

France-Observateur, 1957

The Children of Sputnik Aren't Starry-Eyed

Already the sputniks have been swallowed up by the bogs of literature. We are advised to take religious retreats and do all sorts of other things before we confront outer space, so as to cope with its—grandeur. A steady diet of stupidity is tiring. For that reason we thought it desirable to listen to children discussing the mechanical future of the world—their world. Their literature may be the antidote to that mentioned above.

These children range in age from six to eleven. All believe that the future is a harsh duty, a discipline from which they cannot escape. All agree that the dog sent into outer space suffered a cruel fate. All suffered for her. But it had to be done. These children are heroic rationalists and materialists: the animals are their best friends.

We'll go to the moon because it must be done, because THEY say so.

Q. What is a sputnik?
A. J. M., age 10: It's a rocket. But at school it's an insult.

A. F. A., age 6: It's a round thing that revolves around the earth, the size of a bedroom.

Q. Would you go up in a sputnik?

A. N. R., age 11: Not now, only after they send prisoners up.

A. E. C., age 9: Yes, but not for long. Three days.

A. J. M., age 10: Yes, but not before the third sputnik after the one with the dog.

Q. You know people will soon be going to the moon? Why?

A. F. A., age 6: To make more space.

A. J. M., age 10: Because they think about it all the time, they have rockets on the brain.

A. L. D., age 9: To see the other side of the moon.

A. E. L., age 9: To see the earth from the moon.

Q. Will you go to the moon?

A. All (except J. M.): Yes.

A. J. M.: I have time to decide whether I want to go or not.

Q. Will you spend your vacations there?

A. All: No.

Q. Why won't you spend your vacations there?

A. L. D., age 9: It's not interesting, there's not even any air.

A. E. L., age 9: You can't go for a walk. You have two hundred pounds on your back and all you can see is craters. It's raining meteorites.

A. L. D., age 9: There are no animals, nothing to eat.

A. F. A., age 6: It doesn't make me happy because it's so poor.

Q. Are there things you'd rather see than the moon?

A. F. A., age 6: Russian villages, Hungarian villages, and all that.

A. E. L., age 9: Tahiti, and then the Leeward Islands.

A. N. R., age 11: The bottom of the ocean.

A. J. M., age 10: A planet twice as warm as the moon and with air, where you could go on vacation. But first I want to see the whole world.

A. L. D., age 10: Mars. It has colors and it's more beautiful.

Q. What is beautiful?

A. F. A., age 6: Earth.

Q. What on earth?

A. F. A., age 6: The trees. The houses. The cars. The people.

Q. Grown-ups were all surprised that they managed to launch the sputnik. Were you surprised?

A. J. M., age 10: Not me. It had to happen some day.

A. L. D., age 9: *They* had been talking about it too long already.

A. F. A., age 6: What surprised me is that it was attracted to the earth. They launched it straight up and it started turning around the earth.

Q. Do you think the sputnik moves very fast?

A. All (except F. A.): Yes.

A. F. A., age 6: I think it goes pretty fast.

Q. Is there anything that you find more surprising than the satellite?

A. N. R., age 11: Yes, the tunnels under the English Channel and the Alps.

Q. Was it right to put a dog in the sputnik if they weren't sure that it would live?

A. All: Yes.

Q. What would you do in the sputnik?

A. N. R., age 11: I would count all the dials.

A. E. L., age 9: I would be bored.

A. J. M., age 10: I would take plenty of books that my parents don't let me read at home, like *Les Pieds Nickelés*.

A. F. A., age 6: And if you died, you wouldn't know it, you'd go right on reading.

Q. Do you think it's good or bad to go to the moon and to travel through space?

A. F. A., age 6: It's not good.

A. J. M., age 10: It's good for a little while.

A. N. R., age 11: It's good. But at school there are kids who say that God doesn't want men to change. They say that it shouldn't be allowed.

A. F. A., age 6: It's the head of France who should say whether it's allowed or not.

Q. When you're grown up, would you like to do scientific research? Would you like to build sputniks and rockets?

A. N. R., age 11: No, I wouldn't like that.

A. E. L., age 9: If you make a mistake, it's too serious.

A. F. A., age 6: I would. When I'm grown up I'm going to build rockets to send to the stars.

Q. What do you have to know, what do you have to learn, in order to build rockets?

A. F. A., age 6: You have to know geography. And also you have to watch how mechanics work.

A. J. M., age 10: You have to have so many ideas that you go crazy. Finally you hit on the right one.

Q. What do you think space is like?

A. F. A., age 6: All white.

A. N. R., age 11: All black.

A. E. L., age 9: Like a black mass that glows every two hours.

A. J. M., age 10: Immense, gray, extraordinary, incomprehensible by our brains.

France-Observateur, 1957

When There's Enough for Two, There's Not Necessarily Enough for Three

He had begun by doing a little of this and a little of that. Sometimes it went all right and sometimes it didn't, but he was still young and everybody, they say, has troubles. He was tall, good-looking, knew accounting and English, and had good manners. With the help of yoga he had tamed the serpent of ambition that slept in his bosom; he trained his energy and made himself an efficient worker, a man capable of commanding a good salary. He turned thirty, thirty-five. He went to Indochina and India. At times he believed he had it made. He even had a little free time. It was during this period that he learned yoga. He had a wife and a house in Rosny-sous-Bois.

Then Charles Clément turned fifty. After a valiant war, business turned sour. It was 1946.

His wife, Suzette Yvain, had cancer. His mistress, Félicie Crippa, had no job. He was still in business, selling this and that, nothing in particular. Even though he was still a good salesman, and the yoga helped, luck wasn't with him the way it used to be. The yoga wasn't as useful as in the past.

He wanted good things for both Suzette and Félicie. His double life, which the newspapers call "monstrous," was something he accepted. He didn't shirk his responsibilities. Although he loved Félicie, he sold his luxurious apartment in Chantilly to pay for his wife Suzette's operation.

He found an apartment for Suzette in a modest neighborhood, rue Vercingétorix. Time continued to pass. Charles continued to pay for his wife's care. He sold everything that he had brought back from Indochina and India. And what he didn't sell he pawned.

The Crippa family's ribbon factory wasn't doing well. Suzette wasn't well. And there were fewer valuable objects to sell.

Charles Clément told himself that there were other ways out of his predicament. He could cut his expenses. Logically. Reasonably. In other words, he still had hope. He knew that when there's enough for two, there's not necessarily enough for three. It was time to make a choice. He chose to be one of the two who would remain.

Shortly thereafter he began visiting his mother in Chevreuse every Sunday. He explained to his mother that his wife Suzette was convalescing somewhere in France. That was why he came alone. Regularly he brought two packages with him. Only one was meant for his mother: flowers or roast chicken. Not the other. It takes a long time to dispose of a human body; it's not easy work. Charles made several trips a week.

Then he stopped going to Chevreuse and moved in with Félicie Crippa on the avenue de la République.

By now it was 1956. Charles Clément, alias Charles Crippa, was sixty years old. A man of sixty who goes looking for work is suspect. All the more so in the case of Charles Clément, who, though probably not very intelligent, was a proud man who believed he had known a remarkable past.

The ribbon factory was not doing well. Félicie's mother, who had managed it, was now in a nursing home. Charles Clément went to the pawnbroker, redeemed the items he had pawned, and sold them. Once they were sold he had nothing at all.

Now the yoga proved useless. Age sixty, sixty-one. When there's enough for one there's not necessarily enough for two. Félicie remained.

Charles Clément told himself there was another way out of his predicament. He could reduce his expenses still further. Logically. Reasonably. Time to start over again.

The mystery in cases of this kind is total: Charles Clément loved life. His pleasures were limited to an occasional cappuccino and to interminable walks across Paris, ominous but healthy, extended walks of the sort that elderly people in bit cities are wont to overdo, walks that keep an older person going by providing the occasion for disinterested contemplation of the happiness of others. Nothing but cappuccinos and walks for Charles Clément. Otherwise his life was empty. He packed Félicie in Cérébos salt, whose virtues he was intelligent enough to know. He went on for ten months—long enough to spend the money from the sale of the ribbon factory—still sufficiently in love with life to be pleased with its rewards.

And then it was over. The money from the ribbon factory was gone. The electricity and gas bills were piling up. The price of cappuccino went up. Charles Clément tried to sell his apartment, even though he was still living in it. He accepted deposits. He couldn't sell himself any more. Now he knew his time was up.

One night, after his regular walk, the concierge told him that the electricity and gas had been cut off. Charles Clément counted the money he had left, 1,495 francs, and said, "That's going to be a problem for my heir."

He went out and bought a bottle of cognac for 1,490 francs, then returned to his apartment. At that moment he renounced Hindu philosophy and its transcendental power: he tore, broke, destroyed, or burned (with his usual discretion) anything still valuable enough to haggle over. In a rage over having to die. Even the sheet on which he would lie down to shoot himself in the mouth with a revolver he tore. He left nothing. When there isn't enough for anyone, there isn't enough for anyone. Reasonably, logically, the fact must be admitted.

I have no sympathy for Charles Clément. The only point of this article is to counter the journalistic tendency to find "mystery" in every crime. Nothing could be less mysterious, in my opinion, than the pragmatic logic of Charles Clément.

France-Observateur, 1958

The Gentlemen from the Bus Company

We made Miss T——'s acquaintance a short while ago. Before that we used to see her late at night in a certain bar on the Right Bank.

We asked several times who she was. People said, a teacher of foreign languages. How old? Nobody knew. How long had she been coming there every night? Since World War I. Always to the same bar? Yes, always.

Irish, erect, well-groomed, always wearing the same style of hat, every night for forty-three years Miss T—— had come to that same bar to spend her evenings. During the day she gave lessons in foreign languages. At night she came to the bar for a gin or a stout, or a gin and a stout. Never more than that. Ever since World War I.

Miss T—— never married. Some people remember seeing her ten years ago. Others, last night, remembered her from thirty years ago. She was pretty. She still is.

We, too, fell under the spell of Miss T——'s genuine and in-grained charm. One night we invited her to have a drink with us.

"No," she said, "not unless you're willing to be my guest. If I go to the bar, I go alone. At my age you go to bars alone. If you allow yourself to be taken out, people will get the wrong idea about you. Please don't insist."

Apart from coming to this bar every day since World War I, and apart from her lessons in foreign languages, the difficulties of life in a big city find Miss T—— somewhat unprepared. The patrons of this bar would sooner die than let any harm come to Miss T——. But far from here, from her lair, Miss T——'s behavior might seem strange, her manner might create a false impression, her impeccable speech might pass for eccentricity.

Consider this:

Thirteen months ago Miss T—— was involved in a bus accident and nearly killed. The bus stopped suddenly. Miss T——, as light as a farm girl of sixteen, was thrown forward. She sustained a head injury so serious that she couldn't sleep for several months, found it difficult to eat, and suffered pains in her head, stomach, and shoulder. For months afterward she was unable to give her language lessons.

When she came back to the bar, she was still suffering. Yet never once did she complain, because the driver had "had no choice." She came back. And she stayed in France. It never occurred to her to leave. She resumed her normal life. Her innate cheerfulness, the source of her incomparable charm, carried the day. It was not until twelve months later, to the very day, that she began to have doubts: Wasn't her damage claim against the bus company about to expire? She wrote a letter to "the gentlemen from the Bus Company."

This was how we came to know her.

"Could you tell me, please," she said to the bartender—her very words—"how I can reach the gentlemen from the Bus Company?"

The bartender didn't know. By chance we were there and happened to know the answer. And knowing, too, the proper bureaucratic form of address, we suggested that it might be better to write to the Régie Autonome de Transport Parisien rather than to the "gentlemen from the Bus Company."

Miss T—— was full of unshakable hope.

"Those gentlemen," she said—and again I am quoting her literally—"will understand my position. They will see me. I will be compensated."

We asked why she had waited so long to press her claim. She said that she was Irish, aged, and alone, and added that "one must always spend hours waiting in the offices of insurance companies, and sometimes even then they won't see you. And when you're old, you wait with the elderly. Now I admit that it's rather ridiculous at my age, but I can't stand to be kept waiting. I ask myself: What are you doing there with those old people? I have no answer, so I leave. I thank you just the same. When those gentlemen pay my compensation, we'll celebrate together."

November passed, then December.

"Have you heard anything, Miss T——?"

"Not yet. Imagine. Those gentlemen are very busy. But it won't be long now."

January. Still nothing.

"I've been told that I must expect it to take a long time. But those gentlemen will have to answer me some day. Everyone says that I'm in the right. Wish me luck."

"Good luck."

February. Still nothing?

"I've been told that the French bureaucracy in general is very busy. Those gentlemen are overwhelmed. But when they come to my case, they'll move quickly, you'll see. Wish me luck."

"Good luck."

May I express the hope that the gentlemen in charge of the R.A.T.P. will take note of the unshakable esteem that Miss T—— feels for them and overlook her cheerful patience, for which she is no doubt to blame but which makes her so incomparably charming.

France-Observateur, 1958

Racism in Paris

Marcelle B—— is a waitress in a Left Bank restaurant. The eldest of ten children, she has earned her living in this honorable way for the past ten years. Three Left Bank restaurants employ her either as a regular waitress or as an extra, and she does her work extremely well. A week ago Marcelle B—— was on her way home after work, accompanied by the bartender from the restaurant where she had filled in that night as an extra. It was 1:30 in the morning when they got off the Metro at the station in the Tenth Arrondissement that serves the street where Marcelle B—— has her apartment.

Whether Marcelle B—— and her friend from work were on their way home separately or together was their business and nobody else's, you might think. But you would be wrong.

A police wagon passed our two friends shortly after they left the Metro station. Two policemen got out. The wagon stopped a short way down the street (why?). The two policemen approached.

"Papers, please."

Marcelle B——, waitress, and her friend, the bartender, had

their papers, and everything was in order. Except that Marcelle B—— had not yet reported her "change of residence" to the Tenth Arrondissement. The police asked why. She explained.

"Somebody loaned me an apartment in the Tenth," she said, "but just for a few months. I don't plan to stay here. So I didn't see any reason to report my change of residence."

"Why? Don't you like the neighborhood?" asked the policeman.

"No. Just that it isn't my neighborhood," replied Marcelle B——. "I'm used to the Left Bank. I don't plan to stay here."

"You don't like this neighborhood because you think there are too many of them?"

Marcelle B—— did not answer. Her friend from work is North African.

"Say it," the policeman insisted. "Say that you don't like this neighborhood because there are too many of them."

Neither Marcelle B—— nor her friend answered. The policeman took Marcelle B——'s pocketbook and searched it. Nothing.

"And yet you go walking *with one of them* at one-thirty in the morning?" the policeman said, concluding his lecture.

"You! Come with us."

"Why?"

"Shut your mouth."

They arrested the bartender because he was North African. They held him until four in the morning because he was North African. For three hours the policemen played cards. He waited. Twice, since they had made no charge against him, he said, "Would you please do something about my case?"

A legitimate request, answered the same way both times, because he was North African: "You! Shut your mouth."

As for Marcelle B——, she has discovered that she is now "under surveillance by the police" because she took the last Metro home in the company of an Algerian. Marcelle B. asked me what recourse she had, given that she was completely innocent. I didn't know what to say.

P.S. The person who telephoned me at midnight the last time I dared to speak of "Algerians" and who threatened to "bust my face if I did it again" is kindly requested this time to leave his name.

Move On!

I was passing by the Chamber of Deputies. A crowd had gathered.
A policeman was trying to disperse it.

"Move on!"

I approached the policeman anyhow.

"Could you tell me, please, Officer, why this crowd is here?"

"I'm not asking you to understand," he said, "I'm asking you
to move on!"

I moved on.

The other day I tried to park on a sidewalk where parking
seemed to be allowed. A policeman came out of the shadows.

"Move on!"

"Why, Officer? Please tell me why."

"Because I say so! Move on!"

I didn't move on immediately. Because I have a secret interest
in laconic speech, given that I belong to the more loquacious
branch of society. I persisted: "Officer, could you tell me where I
might have a chance of parking?"

"Wherever you find a place! Move on!"

I moved on. And I thought. And I meditated. And I found a place. And I continued, each time I spoke to them, to take secret delight in their laconic speech, which is becoming more laconic as the amount of automobile traffic increases.

Make no mistake about it: their brevity conceals an intense dream, a dream of moving on. The intensity of this dream is directly proportional to the volume of traffic. Its subject is traffic. The movement of traffic. Let me explain what I mean.

The questions we ask the police, however banal, are always taken amiss (except when we ask directions, which automatically ensures that we will move on), because those questions call for answers, and where there is an answer there is always a chance for dialogue. And dialogue is by nature opposed to moving on. And . . .

"If everybody did that" is the fundamental axiom behind the laconic speech of the police. "Move on!" is what follows from that fundamental axiom. If everybody moved on, there would be no problem.

Put yourself in their place. The number of cars is increasing every day, and so is the number of drivers. The number of policemen is not increasing. They're losing ground daily, and the only way to keep up is to make sure that traffic moves on. So every day they become a little more laconic.

Statistics ought to be kept, for a week, say, recording the most laconic orders given by the Paris police. Perhaps there ought to be a contest. And drivers should be trained first to drop the formulas of politeness from their speech, then the relative pronouns, and then the articles. In the end they can get rid of their automobiles, too.

Or else the cops can get rid of the drivers.

France-Observateur, 1958

Pierre A——, Seven Years and Five Months

Pierre A——, seven years and five months old, is a "remarkable student in all respects." Having skipped two grades he is still first in his class. We thought it important not to know Pierre A—— but to try to understand how he saw his world and the world at large. The interview with Pierre A—— was as frank as possible, as his answers will show—answers that no adult could have given in his place.

Q. Do you think grown-ups are nice to children?
A. They're nice, but only within limits.
Q. Do you feel that grown-ups take sufficient care of you? Your parents, say, and your teachers?
A. It's all right the way it is.
Q. Do you think that school is necessary?
A. It's all right.
Q. What's the use of mathematics?
A. Without mathematics you wouldn't be able to keep your books later on.

Q. What's the good of knowing how to read, in your opinion?

A. So you can read the newspapers.

Q. What about writing?

A. When you have no telephone, writing is good for sending telegrams to the hospital when someone is sick.

Q. What did you do in school this morning?

A. I did a dictation called "First Flowers." I misspelled one word: fragrance.

Q. Do you like spelling?

A. Not very much.

Q. Why not?

A. Too much to remember, not enough thinking.

Q. And math?

A. I like math a lot. It's my favorite subject.

Q. Why?

A. Because it seems hard, but then you look for an answer and you see it and it's easy.

Q. What are you learning now in French history?

A. Julius Caesar and a lot of other kings.

Q. What is the use of studying the history of France?

A. It teaches us how people used to live.

Q. Which are your favorite heroes from French history?

A. Joan of Arc because she saved France and she was so young, and Napoleon because he inspired people to follow him. And also the Greek leaders.

Q. Of all the things you've learned, what has surprised you the most?

A. That fish breathe in the water.

Q. And what else?

A. That eels cross the land to get to the ocean.

Q. What about geography? What surprises you most there?

A. I like the way time is in geography. And the mountains and the volcanoes and the railroads and the highways. And that the wind stops the trains.

Q. And on earth, what surprises you the most?

A. The currents in the oceans.

Q. Think carefully. Don't cars and airplanes and sputniks surprise you? Tell me again what surprises you.

A. The human body. Blood. The heart. How it works, the human body. And also radar. The speed of light. The sunlight takes seven minutes to reach us.

Q. What surprises grown-ups but not kids?

A. Politics.

Q. Is there much difference between a man and an animal?

A. Oh, yes.

Q. What are the differences?

A. Animals have four paws and men have two feet. And then there are animals that eat stones, and they say they even eat alarm clocks. I can't remember which animal it is. Something that sounds like "wig." Men don't eat stones.

Q. Don't you see any other difference between animals and men?

A. No.

Q. You don't think that men are more intelligent than animals?

A. Yes. Men are more intelligent than animals. In animals what I think is not good is the lack of intelligence.

Q. What would you like your little cat to do?

A. I'd like him to speak to me. I'm sorry that he's not as intelligent as I am.

Q. Do you prefer noise or quiet?

A. Quiet. Except for the noise of a party.

Q. Do you want to grow up or stay little?

A. Grow up.

Q. Why?

A. In the first place so I can eat what I want. And in the second place so I can do what I want. But I'll miss my mother from when I was little.

Q. Sometimes, though, don't you wish you could stay little?

A. Yes.

Q. Why?

A. Because when I'm grown up I'll have to take an interest in politics. I'd rather have time to think.

Q. Do you remember when you learned to read?

A. No. But there were mountains of blocks on the carpet.

Q. What do you dream about at night?

A. I dream that the house is on fire. I dream that I'm in a boat and there's a storm. I dream that I'm in school.

Q. What dream do you have most often?

A. That the house is on fire. And also that I'm rich.

Q. What would you do if you became rich? Suddenly?

A. I would buy a palace. And armoires.

Q. What does dying mean to you?

A. You can't go to the country any more.

Q. Why don't children ever behave?

A. You always think you don't have enough time. You hurry too much. You want to go fast so you don't waste time. So then you break things.

Q. Why do you think you never have enough time?

A. I don't know.

Q. Are there things in life that make you sad?

A. Yes, when people die in wars.

Q. And in your French history?

A. No, nothing makes me sad there. But dead people in books, that makes me sad.

Q. When a baby is born, are you happy?

A. Yes.

Q. Why?

A. Because there are more people.

Q. What is the first thing you think about in the morning when you wake up?

A. School. You mustn't be late.

Q. What time of day do you like best?

A. Around two-thirty in the afternoon, a half-hour *before* recess.

Q. What stories do you like best?

A. Funny ones.

Q. And what else?

A. Scary ones.

Q. And what else?

A. Stories that make you cry.

Q. Do you ever read the newspaper?

A. Sometimes, a little bit.

Q. What, exactly?

A. The stories at the bottom of the page, and the crimes. But never politics.

Q. Did you like it better when you were very small, or now?

A. Now. On the playground I used to be knocked around by the big kids.

Q. I'd like to ask you one last question. What can't you understand no matter how hard you try? Of all the things you learn about in school.

A. That the earth turns. I can't understand that at all.

France-Observateur, 1958

Paris, August Sixth

In Paris the weather is mostly cloudy with occasional clearing. The temperature is steady. At night women are wearing wool jackets. Last Friday radioactive rain fell on the capital. Or so they say. Nothing is certain. At two in the afternoon Paris became as dark as at ten in the evening. The lights had to be turned on. But the sun reappeared. The censor decided not to talk about it, since for the past two months French routines have been sufficiently disrupted that talk of a "natural" disaster would add undue stress.

Parisians, at this moment the population of your city is probably about one-third of normal.* Just about equal to the population that made the revolution of 1789.

Three days ago ten thousand Renault workers took to the highways. The exodus is still going on and will continue until Au-

---

*Paris is virtually closed down during August, the traditional vacation month in France.—Trans.

gust 15, which is of course a national event. Thousands of photographs will be taken that day in the place de la Concorde and sent all around the world. Photographs of the void. Of policemen yawning at intersections. Only the *bateaux-mouches*, filled to the gunwales with Swedish tourists, will continue to make their way across the abandoned capital, and the elevators of the Eiffel Tower, packed with Germans, will ascend through the pure air of a city become improbable, unreal, uncertain.

The News Never Rests

You have to walk a mile for a loaf of bread or a pack of cigarettes. On the other hand it takes only twelve minutes to get to the Arc de la Triomphe, compared with forty-five minutes a few weeks ago. There is room on the Champs-Elysées. You can go to the movies, see *Mon Oncle*, and park your car.

"Is it Sunday?" asked a child yesterday afternoon, a child from Réaumur, one of the eighty thousand children who never go on vacation. Another, older child explained that it was better than Sunday, it was vacation. And the little child looked with amazement at his four hundred square feet of park—his Mediterranean, his bonbon, his summer.

With its population reduced to what it was at the time of the Revolution, Paris is quiet. Paris has ceased to exist. It has gone elsewhere. It is somewhere between Troyes, Remiremont, and the Cévennes. In Spain, apparently, people are cramming the beaches. A certain segment of Paris is in Saint-Tropez. Including Brigitte Bardot. What would she do in Troyes? If Brigitte Bardot were in Troyes, she wouldn't be Brigitte Bardot, and I don't mean that she would be incognito. You can't go incognito without cooperation between the thing fled and the person fleeing. Not with you, but not without you. It's the same for everybody. People go to Saint-Tropez to escape from Paris, provided they find Paris there when they arrive, Paris and its tastes, forgotten for just an instant. They go to dance the gallopade at Palmyre's, where the French intelligentsia disports itself. Paris goes to be seen dancing by its idols, in itself an effective education in the ways of the world. I say this with no pejorative intention. It's just that my curiosity increases with each passing year. Ten years and every day of summer the same tune, a gallopade so easy to dance to, amazes the French intelligence.

If you want details about who goes and who stays, here they are. All of Auteuil has gone. Everybody. Everybody from the boulevard Saint-Germain as well. The folks from Montreuil are the least likely to depart. And once you get out as far as Versailles, nobody goes at all, except for the bourgeoisie. The concierges go away for only seventeen days, nobody knows why. That's just the way it is. The people in the food trade go for a month. Certain bakeries close for a month and a half. The fashionable shops have sales. They do a land-office business. Frightful as it is, they're already photographing the fall models. The Chamber of Deputies is closed for reasons of its own. But a guard, a so-called Republican Guard, protects it from overly curious Americans—overly curious about the French revival. Certain professions, like schoolteachers, are nowhere to be found in the capital. Certain others, like policemen, can't afford the luxury. Twenty-four people were arrested last week, and the newspapers announced the event with obvious satisfaction that life goes on.

An Abandoned Capital

As reported in *France-Soir,* a group of French gentlemen, disguised as house painters (pistols in hand), seized a group of rebels belonging to the [Algerian] National Liberation Front, who were meeting in the apartment of the "self-styled filmmaker" Cécile Decugis. Plain to see, the news never rests, and journalists whose beat is the prefecture of police (*préfecturiers* in the argot of the trade) don't forget, come summertime, the habits they've acquired working with the police during the rest of the year. Like spitting in the faces of people the police have arrested. As for Cécile Decugis, the "self-styled filmmaker," I saw her working last month in Monte Carlo for Brigitte Bardot's producer, Raoul Levy. It happens that Cécile Decugis is indeed an accredited film professional, a member of the guild with all her professional credentials in order. She is a film editor. Just as a set-up man at Renault is a set-up man at Renault.

Other Paris news: the cafe waiters, tired of speaking Swedish, are eager for the return of their regulars.

Still other news: all the museums are open. By five in the afternoon the heat is as heavy as in the caves at Lascaux.

Still more news: as they've done every year since the German occupation, the paulownias of the quays of Paris are trying to bloom again. Their annual desire to bloom is troubling. Will they make it this year? Who knows? Since they were planted they bloomed only during the German occupation. Why? For one reason: because in those days the air was stiflingly pure.

France-Observateur, 1958

Seine-et-Oise, My Country

There are two thousand of us, if you count those who have second homes here. Otherwise there are precisely 1,813 residents of Neauphle-le-Château.

Neauphle is one of the finest towns in the Seine-et-Oise. It is built on a promontory that stretches northward toward the Eure and the valley of the Mauldre and whose heights are swallowed up to the south and east by the forest of Rambouillet and the former royal forests of Versailles. Two dreadful national highways, the N12 and N191, pass close to Neauphle but fortunately skirt the center of town, about a mile off. On weekend nights rivers of light flow past Neauphle, yellow on Sunday nights, red on Saturdays. From the intensity of the luminous floods that roll over the hillsides Neauphle knows whether the weekend has been good or bad. Sometimes, in June, the wave of light comes to a standstill, forming a compact mass with a gap. Then the Neauphleans who are watching say, "Oh, those poor Parisians!" When a Neauphlean leaves Neauphle, he always goes against the tide; he goes into Paris, but only on Saturday or Sunday.

As I was saying, we number two thousand. The contractors are all Italians, the florist is from the Sarthe, the gardener from the Loiret, the mechanic from Warsaw, the shoestore owner from Saône-et-Loire; there are Spaniards, Angevins, and Algerians. The native Neauphleans number ten. All live cheek by jowl in a residential community known since the French Revolution as Neauphle-la-Montagne but today called Neauphle-le-Château, one of the seven hundred incorporated towns in the Seine-et-Oise district.

There are rabbits all around, and hedgehogs. Now and then a hedgehog, leaving the royal forest of Versailles, which stands between us and Paris, laboriously climbs the avenue de la République Française. I saw one that made it alive to within fifty yards of the war memorial. That was a weekday like any other, during the summer.

If the forest stands at the gates of Neauphle, it is Grand Marnier that stands at its heart, as it has done for more than a century. The work of making the orange-flavored liqueur is not difficult: eighty young women from the town are employed in the Grand Marnier factory, whose owner, Monsieur Lapostolle, never makes more than a brief stop in Neauphle.

An Airplane Factory

Deana Durbin, Charles David, François Peugeot, André Mandouze, and various assorted industrialists, writers, journalists, notaries, and financiers make up the bulk of the people with second homes here, most of them located either in the section known as Petit Nice or along the same avenue de la République Française that the hedgehog so laboriously climbed. Don't try to meet one of these "secondary residents." You'll never succeed. The secondary resident is Neauphle's mortal illness. He occupies three-quarters of the town's built-up area. But he's never there. The engaging Monsieur Perier, mayor of Neauphle, and his city council devote most of their efforts to the fight against the absenteeism of the secondary resident. They wage a roundabout but nonetheless energetic struggle—roundabout because there is of course no way to force anyone to live in Neauphle. To restore the local population to three thousand, the city council has issued permits for the construction of three hundred three-story dwelling units and twenty-four individual homes over the next three years. At Les Gâtines, also over the next three years, Marcel Dassault plans to build an airplane factory that will employ 2,500 workers. Neauphle will be saved.

Neauphle will be saved and ruined. With its three thousand residents Neauphle will within a decade link up with its neighboring towns Bois-d'Arcy, Les Clayes, Plaisir, and Petits-Prés and become one of the suburbs of Paris.

Over the past four years the price of land has doubled.

We're just over twenty-three miles from Saint-Germain-des-Prés. In forty minutes you can be at the Cercle Elégant, in fifty minutes at the place de la République. Of those twenty-three miles only about eight and a half are still dark at night: the superhighway is lighted by giant lamps.

I like Neauphle. I had no home and now I have one. A funny little place, which is what a home should always be. For in Neauphle no one is from Neauphle, nobody knows anybody else, nobody invites anybody over, nobody likes anyone, and nobody hates anybody.

The real Neauphleans left when we moved up from the Loiret and Piémont, and those of us who moved in never introduced ourselves. The Neauphleans of 1962 are looking forward to better times ahead. They want homes they can leave to go somewhere else and then return to when they're done. With birds in the trees Neauphle is too sad, they say, to be bearable for long. In other words, the Neauphlean does not know that Neauphle is sad because of him. He lives in a void of his own devising, but he does not know it. His city stands in his way and causes him to suffer. If there were no place else, he tells himself, life here would be unbearable, but fortunately there are other places, relatives in Dieppe, say, or Carcassonne. An illusion of distant relations, which makes Neauphle, my home in the Seine-et-Oise, a place where every act, word, or deed carries with it an echo, a chance of insidious or sudden metamorphosis. A child's cry. Peonies stunningly in bloom. Cold. Fog on the Mauldre. The return of the cats at dusk.

The fatherland of anxiety, of the "gray mouse" that here shows its nose.

No More Farmers

Neauphle always makes me want to stop talking—Neauphle where I have never spoken to anyone.

Fifty years ago this was a large commercial town where the big farmers of the region came for supplies. There are no more farmers. The Parisians came. Then, as the number of automobiles increased, Neauphle became a vacation spot. People remember when vacationers came for two months at a time. Now it's just a weekend spot. During the summer the avenue de la République is deserted. We are on the Côte d'Azur.

Once I drove twenty-five miles out of Neauphle—it was eleven at night—looking for a pack of cigarettes. I found one in a service station at midnight.

On Saturday night, the Balto, a cafe and tobacconist's shop on the main square, stays open unusually late. On other days Neauphle is asleep by nine o'clock. On Saturdays in front of the Balto there are motorcycles. In Seine-et-Oise young people spend their Saturday nights looking for open cafes. There's one in Beynes, one in Neauphle, one out on the highway near Pontchartrain. An open cafe is a party. Ours in Neauphle has a pool table and a jukebox with waltzes for the tramps. The owners always keep a nice dance-hall number in the jukebox for the tramps. Around midnight, one of these tramps, Coco, Italian by birth, who winter or summer always wears a cap and boots, is dancing. After quaffing his tenth glass of wine he dances alone in front of the jukebox. In the four years I've been watching he's always been dancing alone. The young people don't look at him any more. Nor do they pay any attention to another tramp, an old, defrocked priest who's been hanging around for fifteen years and who doesn't need any wine to start in reciting the mass in Latin. When Coco and his companion get out of hand—Coco because waltzing makes him dizzy and he starts overturning tables, the priest because his recital becomes deafening when he reaches the Elevation—somebody asks them nicely to leave. Coco and his companion never cause trouble. Monday morning, red-nosed, they're there, on time.

When I came to Neauphle four years ago, I thought there were a lot of lunatics in the town. But it was the tramps I was afraid of, and since then I've come to know them. The man who wears a top hat and a red carnation and who in fair weather can be seen crossing the empty squares is crazy but not dangerous. He comes from Charcot's Asylum in Plaisir. Every year he finds a new generation of kids to entertain.

Triumph of the void. Early to bed and early to rise, Neauphleans want mainly to pass unnoticed. They read the *Parisien libéré*. The Neauphlean, to hear him tell it, is completely apolitical.

Last December, at eleven o'clock at night, our friend André Mandouze was attacked with plastic explosive.

The next day people were talking about it in Paris, but not in Neauphle.

Of four hundred newspapers sold each day, two hundred are *Parisiens libérés*. Reading a paper like that, you don't get all hot and bothered. Here the 170 registered Communist voters read the *Parisien libéré*.

Nails

A few weeks ago somebody scattered nails over the main square near where it joins the place aux Herbes.

The next day nobody talked about it. "Maybe it was some kids," was all they said.

Secret Army Organization slogans started to appear on the walls of the Grand Marnier plant.* They stayed up.

Although there are 170 registered Communist voters, only ten copies of *Humanité* [the Communist party newspaper] are sold each day, and eight copies of *Libération*. Those papers are bought in Paris, where a fair percentage of Neauphle's workers go to work. The *Observateur* you ask somebody else to buy for you. Other newspapers are not much read. Only the *Parisien libéré* is bought publicly.

Nights in Neauphle-le-Château are almost always peaceful, disturbed only by the buses leaving for Paris at seven in the morning, and in the summer by the birds at daybreak. Those are

---

*The Secret Army Organization was a group of military officers opposed to the French decolonization of Algeria. It was responsible for numerous terrorist attacks and assassinations in the late 1950s. —Trans.

the only sounds one hears along this irreproachably straight avenue of political despair: the avenue de la République Française, where we rich folk congregate (as well as over in Petit Nice)—the same avenue that the hedgehog climbed, foolishly in the eyes of some.

It's down that street that "they" come by night. They have intelligence agents in Neauphle. There are people who know which agents fingered our friend Mandouze, among other things.

But at daybreak we wave hello to one another, we wave hello to them. They are affable men, these murderers, with the pleasant air of people with roots in the community. They know they're safe where they are. Here no one will point them out on the streets. Anybody who knows the secret is in on the crime: a sterile form of knowledge.

There hasn't been a crime in Neauphle in ten years. Except for the bungled attempt on the life of our friend Mandouze.

Sometimes, in the morning, you hear footsteps from the avenue de la République Française. Housewives returning from the market, with copies of the *Parisien libéré* sticking out of their baskets. That's it for the day. People die once. They go out one time and then they have the garden and the newspaper and the television.

From "La Pierre Sauteuse" to Les Sablons not a store is open between noon and two o'clock; the streets are deserted. Occasionally you see a dog.

The only thing that everybody agrees Neauphle needs is a movie theater.

"Neauphle must be saved from nonexistence," as the mayor puts it.

Only one way to do that, the mayor knows, and we all agree: bring in enough workers to change the nature of life in Neauphle, which for the moment is nonexistent or inert.

What I've said in this essay holds true for all the towns in Seine-et-Oise that are not mere suburbs of Paris. Neauphle lacks intellectual courage and passion for want of anything to apply it to, which is the same as saying that the Neauphlean does not yet exist. He is still someone who comes from Dieppe or Saumur or Udine. What he has in common with his neighbor is some nice lilacs or a good apple tree. The surrounding countryside is extraordinary. Alain Resnais wanted to film the Nevers sequences of *Hiroshima mon amour* here.

This is built-up country, though, defended fiercely, they say, during the Hundred Years War. Its castle rivals that of Montfort (how I dislike Montfort!). There's nothing to say but how sorry I am that Neauphle is this way and how sorry I am that it will be the same, in a different way, tomorrow. It's best not to think about it.

France-Observateur, 1962

Nadine from Orange

After the "interrogation" of André Berthaud was broadcast on television, I went to see his wife. I stood at her door for an hour. She didn't want to let me in. She asked me to leave. She was terrified. But finally she agreed to see me. We talked for a long time. As we spoke she listened to the sounds from the stairway: the police again. The image comes back to me: the man in the station house on the rue des Saussaies, back to the wall, floodlights shining in his face, the police barking at him, the priest—they carved him up as though he were the main dish at a banquet. You're going to admit it, right? Admit it. Admit that you touched her. Bastard. Eighteen years later, that image stays with me—unbearable. He asked to go to the bathroom and there plunged a knife into his heart. He who knew nothing knew how to do that. I remember the effect of the news when it was broadcast that same night on television. I remember how angry people were, and how they refused to be manipulated, refused to swallow the police version that André Berthaud committed suicide for no other reason than because he was guilty. A disaster for the police, that case.

Now as then, when the events took place, I see Berthaud's gesture not as his only way out but as a refusal to take part in the deadly comedy staged by the police. In this instance his mental incapacity served him well: he chose his own death. That night, for some strange reason, the police station was suddenly empty. There was no more "work" to do, the police were alone, they had been "taken in," they said, "fooled": the man was dead. The love between the man and the child would remain unpunished; death had put an end to it. I absolutely believe in that love. André Berthaud and the little girl loved each other.

The medical examiner's report was categorical: little Nadine had not been raped. A rape might have occurred, but in fact it did not occur. It is possible, even likely, that the rape that was never committed was displaced onto André Berthaud's final act: a love so violent cannot exist without this consequence of desire. But the rape never took place, I think, because of the strength of the child's love.

It's none of my business, none of anybody's business. The rape did not occur.

Suddenly I realize how peculiar it is that the men who murdered four police officers last month (November 1979) were arrested within forty-eight hours, while three and a half months after the crime the murderers of Pierre Goldman have still not been found.*

Q. How did it all start?
A. Nadine's cousins were friends of my daughter, Danièle. That's how my husband and Nadine met. They all saw each other during vacations at Notre-Dame-des-Monts. People think that they had known each other a long time, but that's not true. Nadine and André did not meet until the end of our vacation, between August 31 and September 4. It was during those five days that they became friends.

---

*Pierre Goldman was a criminal and ex-convict who was murdered shortly after a book he wrote about his life attracted much favorable attention in literary circles. The crime was never solved. —Trans.

Q. What happened between September 4 and Tuesday the twenty-sixth, when André left home?

A. He went back to Notre-Dame-des-Monts for three days without us, to see Nadine.

Q. During the five days of vacation, while you were at Notre-Dame-des-Monts, what happened?

A. They fell for each other and became fast friends. The newspapers didn't tell the whole truth. The little girl couldn't live without André any more than he could live without her. Wherever we went, she showed up. They played together and swam together. She threw her arms around his neck and went into the ocean with him, like that, hanging on around his neck. She rode on his shoulders. The minute she woke up in the morning she came looking for him. We thought it was funny, even annoying. Once she came to our house and he left with her to go swimming at a place two miles away. I should have gotten angry and stopped him from walking two miles just to be with her. Wherever we went she showed up. She ran away from her grandmother's and came to be with André. She would have slept and eaten her meals in our house if she could have. Wherever we went she found us. Once we went for a picnic in the woods and she found us. André was sleeping. We told her to go away. But then André woke up and of course he insisted that she stay with us.

Q. How was André Berthaud with his own children?

A. He loved all three of us terribly, in his own way. He would have killed anyone who touched his children. But I must say that he never showed an interest in any child, never, like the interest he showed in Nadine—not even his own children. Never had I seen him like that. With Nadine it was a sudden thing. He made a great fuss over her from the first time he saw her. You have to say he was sick. He was a very violent man, a very simple man, for whom everything was a life or death matter. The story of him and Nadine was the story of a child of twelve who falls for another child of twelve. Never could I have imagined such a thing. When we left Notre-Dame-des-Monts it was an awful scene. She wanted to stay with him, and he wanted to stay with her. They were both crying. They were desperate.

Q. You said that he went back to see her one weekend. And that it was after that three-day weekend with Nadine that you began to worry.

A. Yes. He wanted to see Nadine again. He kept repeating, "I want to see Nadine again." He was constantly talking about the child. He wanted photos of her everywhere, on the television set, on the mantelpiece, everywhere. We tried to take them away. It was then that he began to threaten us, to threaten our daughter, Danièle. "If you take away a single photo of Nadine," he said, "Danièle will never see J—— again." (J—— is Danièle's fiancé.)

Q. Do you think that the fact that Danièle went with him to Orange—

A. Yes, I'm sure of it. I'm sure he said, "If you don't come with me, you will never see J—— again."

Q. Tell me a little more about the period before the decision to go away with Nadine.

A. He wanted to see Nadine again, desperately. He spoke to me about it. "I want to see Nadine. You don't have to be jealous of Nadine. I love her deeply. If she were fifteen or sixteen, I would understand if you were jealous, but Nadine, you don't have to be jealous of her." I didn't worry at first because Nadine was 500 miles away.

Q. What did you worry about?

A. I was just afraid that he would go and bother the little girl's parents, upset them with his trying to see her, and that they would throw him out. I was never afraid of anything else.

Q. Did his passion for Nadine grow as time passed?

A. Yes. We tried to help him get over it, the kids and I. Nadine is a lovely little girl. But we told him, "Nadine has dark skin, she's losing her teeth, she's ugly." He got into terrible rages. "There's no one more beautiful," he said. Toward the end, in the days before September 26, it was terrible. He stopped sleeping. He stopped eating. He thought of nothing but the girl. We tried to get him to smile, we asked him to smile. He couldn't do it. "If I could see Nadine," he said, "things would be better. If I could see Nadine again, I'd get over it."

Q. By then nothing else mattered to him?

A. No, nothing. He paid no attention to us. But even before, after we came back from Notre-Dame-des-Monts, nothing else mattered to him. For example, his son, Claude, who is twelve, he wanted to make him a bicycle racer. He had bought him all this fantastic equipment. Every Sunday for years he went to watch Claude train in the park at Vincennes. He loved it. But after meeting Nadine, he never went again, not once. It hurt Claude. I remember that at Notre-Dame-des-Monts, Claude tried to chase Nadine away. He even hit her sometimes to get her to go away. He was jealous, as you might expect. But the girl always stayed, and André always went looking for her. Nothing could keep them apart.

Q. You weren't worried while you were still on vacation?

A. No, not then, not yet. It was annoying, exasperating, to see them together all the time not paying attention to anybody else, but that was all. It was after our return, especially after the weekend, that things got out of hand for André, and he was overwhelmed by a passion he couldn't do anything about. And I was afraid.

Q. You never had any doubts about the nature of André Berthaud's passion for Nadine?

A. Never. People have evil minds. They don't understand. Since a lot of children are raped, they said this was a case of child rape. But look, even though I never saw anything of the kind, never imagined anything of the kind, I knew that this was something else, something completely different.

Q. What?

A. Impossible to say. Words are inadequate. Love, yes, but not simply the love of a man for a woman or of a father for a child. Something different. I can't explain.

Q. You were never afraid for Nadine?

A. Never. I never saw the least bit of sadism in André's passion for Nadine. Never. When the detectives came, I told them not to worry, I swore that André would never harm a hair on Nadine's head. Even though I'd never seen anything like the passion that Nadine and André felt for each other, I knew that it would never have occurred to my husband to harm the child in any way. Never.

You understand, he was a little simple. A very good man—
he'd give you the shirt off his back—but because he was very
simple he was rejected somewhat by his neighbors, his family,
our friends. And when he met the little girl, and she was so nice
to him, and looked for him all the time, and was so sweet, he
was overwhelmed. She kissed him the way she kissed her father. Her arms were around his neck all day long. In my opinion she was a child who never enjoyed the benefit of having a
father. Her father is a military pilot and she practically never
saw him. Her behavior was also unusual. At first I thought the
whole thing was odd. Now I can understand it a little. Perhaps
they needed each other. It was a sudden thing. From the moment they met they couldn't live without each other. They were
carried away. Nobody had ever cared for either of them the way
they cared for each other.

Q. What kind of man was André Berthaud?

A. A very simple man, as I said before, like a twelve-year-old
child. A very good man. The son of divorced parents—he was
raised by his grandmother. A stubborn man. Sometimes he had
incredible rages, so incredible that if the detectives had come
and told me he'd killed somebody in an argument, I wouldn't
have been surprised. But Nadine—never, never, he would
never have done her harm. What he liked best was sports and
nature. He was a man who never smoked, never drank alcohol,
never drank anything but milk. Every Sunday we went to the
woods in Sénart or to the park at Vincennes. He was a man who
picked flowers, if you see what I mean. I was too lazy to bend
down to pick them, but not him. He never got tired of picking
flowers.

Q. The woods at Sénart—isn't that where he took Nadine?

A. Yes. You know I have my own ideas about what they were
doing in that forest. He must have gone there to pick flowers, and
he probably told her stories, kid stories. He loved kid stories.

Q. After his return to Notre-Dame-des-Monts did he write to
Nadine?

A. I think so. Yes. He wrote her letters. I never saw them.

Q. Did you ever discuss suicide with him?

A. Of course, the way everybody does. He never understood

suicide. He said that suicide required extraordinary courage, which he couldn't understand.

Q. I have friends who were watching television that night, who saw how he was insulted and treated by the cops.

A. I never saw it. People told me that he was up against the wall in the light of the floodlights and that they shouted at him, "All right, admit it, you touched her, you bastard." They say that everybody insulted him and he said nothing, and that he looked terrible, just terrible. I think he killed himself because they said he was a criminal, they said that he touched Nadine, even though it never occurred to him to touch Nadine, never, I could swear it, and he never understood that people, with their evil minds, could accuse him of such a thing without any proof, and even put the idea into his head. It drove him mad. I'd like to do something. I'd like to bring suit against the people who drove him to do such a thing. Do you think I can?

Q. I don't think so. But I advise you to try anyway.

A. I'd like you to say something about my daughter, Danièle, who is in prison in the Vaucluse. I get letters from the warden and from others in the workhouse where they have her. They all say that Danièle is a fine girl, a hard worker, and that they're prepared to do whatever they can to get her out of there. She was just a child, Danièle. She loved her father, and she was also afraid that he was going crazy, and she was afraid that he would stop her from seeing J——, the boy she loves.

Q. Was André Berthaud strict with his daughter?

A. Very strict. She's a girl of eighteen and a half who had never been to a dance. Not once. He wouldn't allow it. He wanted her to be what she is, hardworking. To tell the truth, she was afraid of him. And she wanted to please him. She didn't see any harm in going to look for Nadine, because the way she's been brought up, she's just a little girl herself. She had gone off before with her father to move furniture, once in Champagne, once in the suburbs. I wasn't worried. André was never very nice to his daughter. He was to his son, Claude, but not to Danièle. She tried to be nice to him, though.

Q. What do you think would have happened if André Berthaud hadn't seen Nadine again?

A. I don't know. Perhaps in time he would have forgotten about her. But I'm not sure. I don't know.

Q. If the cops hadn't forced him to commit suicide, he would have been in jail for at most six months. Did you know that?

A. I know it. People have told me. But what can I do?

France-Observateur, 1961

Trash and Stick Are Slated to Die

On 22 December 1956 the bodies of two young men were found in the park at Saint-Cloud. Both had been shot with a revolver. Three weeks later, Jean-Claude Vivier and Jacques Sermeus, both age nineteen, were arrested for robbery and possession of weapons.

Trash, also known as Pumpkin-head, and his pal Stick were sentenced to die at age twenty on the first day of spring 1958, four years after their release from the orphanage of Saint Bernadette at Andaux.

Here is news of them, passed on to me by Vivier's attorney, Maître Planty.

They're together now, in the same cell at La Santé Prison, just as they were in the orphanage. Sermeus is afraid of dying. This annoys Vivier, but he consoles his friend anyway. Vivier still hopes that he won't have to die. Yesterday they signed a petition for their appeal. But their lawyer, Planty, doesn't hold out much hope. They don't yet understand. They complain that they haven't slept well for the past two nights because a light is always kept burning in the cells of death row prisoners. They hadn't been aware of this. It surprises them. They would like to get a good night's sleep. They remain in what the journalists and spectators at Versailles unanimously denounced as a state of utter depravity. Journalists, judges, and the general public can therefore remain calm; the fear of death that the two condemned men will soon feel—very soon, at dawn—will be an animal fear, a fear that, "oddly enough, does not move," a fear that "has no rhyme or reason," an "absurd" fear—to borrow a few phrases from my fellow journalists—*a fear that will frighten no one but themselves,* when the time comes to experience it.

It's all over, then. Before long nobody will care about this case. Since these are not dogs, the S.P.C.A. will not lift a finger to help. Yet when the dog catcher picks up strays and takes them to the gas chamber, it seems that the dogs sense something and howl and have to be calmed down. But the S.P.C.A. won't lift a finger unless the victims are dogs, duly certified as dogs. So no one will witness the fear of the condemned men, neither dog nor man. Except, in the latter category, perhaps, Maître Floriot, who in good society bears the sobriquet the Widow because of his constant concern for orphans. We advice him, in any case, to go watch the two heads fall into the sawdust, so that later, when a case requires it, he can mimic the cruel phases of the execution, of animal death.

During the trial seventy-five journalists found that Trash, so called because at the orphanage he ate everything, including cheese crusts and bread crumbs, and Stick, whose name comes from his "innately" slender build, were strangely devoid of charm, lacking the slightest attractive quality.

The journalists claimed that the passing of the death sentence left them indifferent.

The journalists unanimously found that the defendants' inability to express themselves, their incoherent statements, their lack of grammar, their bearing in the witness box, their dress, their shaving of their mustaches, their eyes, their tears, their lack of tears, their feet, and a hundred other things all told against them.

"What did you plan to do with the guns?" asked Judge Chapar, president of the court.

"Holdups," Vivier answered.

Whereupon the judge remarked: "When they carry revolvers, they're not going hunting."

Do you suppose that either of these "hoodlums" smiled at this judicious observation by the presiding judge, so judicially necessary at this moment in the proceedings? No. Nothing.

"The guns were for holdups," Sermeus ominously repeated, instead of remarking, for instance, that people don't hunt with revolvers.

"Fifty days ago?" is what Desnoyers, alias Father d'Uruffe, might have answered.

"I don't know. I no longer know. I'm no longer the same man."

But those two—they had changed and didn't even know it! Desnoyers was fully aware that he had changed, and so were his judges. He committed his double crime alone, at an adult and responsible age. Later, his double alibi permitted him to suffer (as he worked a crucifix in his hands), to suffer both for the man he was and for his brother in religion, the priest he also was, to suffer in such an obvious way that it was considered more expedient, a worse punishment, to allow him to continue to suffer on earth rather than reward him with a redeeming death in heaven. Et cetera.

As a result of which, indeed *fortunately,* Desnoyers was still able, as recently as ten years ago, to scamper about among us, still able to attract the attention of the press, the famous, and even, perhaps, of the Church, of which he was one of the most indubitable martyrs. Good work, Desnoyers! Good work! Alive? Present, yes.

But for the other two, no hope. At the orphanage in Auteuil they should have taught them the power of the word and the rhetorical use of the caesura rather than gardening and the shoemaker's trade. The psychiatrists of course have found their mental ages to lie somewhere between eleven and fifteen. No matter. An attempt should have been made to make their degradation moving, to paint them as fallen angels with voice, gesture, and word. In court such tactics are always useful. I'm afraid that there are major gaps in the education of Trash and Stick.

"You were wearing gloves. Why?"

"It was winter," answered Sermeus.

Such platitudes are disturbing, even to the court. A hundred other answers should have been given before that one—even if I can't think of one right away. How about: "And you, Monsieur le Président, in winter don't you wear gloves?" A little comic relief for the audience would have served better. And who knows?

No. A being, a human being come to think of it, whose rhetorical ability is nonexistent, whose capacity to argue remains at a "digestive" level, is a nullity, is human only in the most comical sense. The spectators in the courtroom at Versailles had no sympathy for those two. Let them grow up in La Santé. Since they didn't die of scarlet fever at the age of nine or ten, they are subject to the jurisdiction of the cleaver that will soon plunge into the quick of their absurd childhoods. Epiphenomena of a society that is trying with all its might to be classless, Trash and Stick are such obvious and striking illustrations of the refusal of "certain social strata" to fall in with our efforts that it is only normal that we should eliminate them. That's the way it is.

"I was afraid to say, Hands up!" said Sermeus.

"But you weren't afraid to kill them," shot back Judge Chapar.

Judge Chapar's son would have said "Hands up!" He wouldn't have said "to stick leeks," he would have said "to plant leeks," even if Judge Chapar had sent him to the Saint Bernadette orphanage to learn shoemaking. What's happening to the language? If murderers are no longer charming, if they no longer move us, what sort of mess is crime in? And as for the Widow, the pride of our drawing rooms, isn't it a pity that the audience for his pleas, for his hypocritical reenactment of the murders (unanimously hailed in the press as "stunning," stunning and necessary so that the parents of the victims could cry fresh tears and faint in court), is limited to the courtroom?

No. Let these people go back where they came from: the void. Society will congratulate itself for performing this act of cleansing, this ritual of so-called social hygiene.

France-Observateur, 1958

Horror at Choisy-le-Roi

"Beware! Beware! Much ink has been spilled over this nameless, inexcusable crime. Let us turn a deaf ear to the lament of the aesthetes over the crime of love. . . ."

L'Aurore, 4 June

Bogus explanations have been put forward for the crimes of Simone Deschamps and Dr. Evenou. Their bank accounts and marriage contracts have been scrutinized, and yielded nothing. Some have blamed passion: Evenou was trying to get rid of his wife, they say. But this, too, has proved false. So people will no doubt go on looking, go on searching for common motives for this crime, go on trying to "classify" it, because outside the accepted categories of crime our minds feel uneasy.

It will be difficult but probably someone will succeed, let us hope without resorting to the mechanistic, jesuitical kinds of reasoning with which one can explain anything and everything.

One can't, of course, explain what is obscure, but one can attempt to circumscribe the darkness, to leave in the shadows only what is shadowy by nature.

The whole business is hardly off page one, but I think that one can say this much: if Evenou did experience true "passion" with his mistress, Simone Deschamps, he did not love her. Something quite different from love was involved: an eroticism that, like love, careens from one extreme to another, in this case carried to the nth degree. I love you, therefore I hate you, therefore I am going to kill you. With her he experienced sex unlike any he had ever experienced in his life, but as he said, he never would have married her. He wanted her for a secret part of his life; like a pure vice she could not be openly avowed. But their affair had been going on for seven years, and was progressing. As this secret affair slowly neared its end, it refused to die, it insisted on a climax. Disaster hovered in the air.

Last Friday night, this woman, this ugly, elderly woman, decked out in an erotic costume, naked under her black cloak, wearing black gloves and armed with a dagger, not only crossed the threshold of crime but played out the last act of her love. She loved him. She loved him so much that she made herself and her love over as he wanted them. Although it is difficult to separate a crime like this from its emotional context, it is tempting to try. The staging of the crime is astonishing—astonishing for its clear meaning. Evenou gave his mistress the illusion of freedom. But she was not taken in. She waited for the telephone call and alone, at midnight, climbed the three flights of stairs that separated her from her crime and his death. And he waited for her *as though she could have pulled back*, as though she were free either to stop loving him or to go on loving him. Thus she went to the scene of the crime—the atrocious, barbarous crime—as a young girl goes to her first date. For even as their passion was ending, she felt rejuvenated, for the last time. He made her dress like a stripper—for one man only—he who had known her for seven years; neither of them was capable of anything more. And after he had embraced her and said goodbye to her, he pointed to the place of her crime, to his heart, again, *as though she did not know.*

Of course there was premeditation. It had been going on for seven years. But the term *premeditation* is inadequate once the sexual need has reached such heights that an end is the only way out. To repeat, if she loved him, she had pretended not to love him, as he wished—love had been humbled by sexual need. She obeyed his wishes by poisoning herself for a month—of her own "free" will. And while he, in a perfect parody of divinity, awaited her in his wife's bedroom, she behaved exactly as though he governed her fate; right to the very end she played the slave, the subject of this horrible would-be God—of whom she was not afraid.

The shadows, I think we must admit, are "real."* I think we must kill (since we do kill) the criminals of Choisy, but we should abandon once and for all any attempt to interpret the shadows— it cannot be done in the light of day. The error of the newspapers is naive: What does it mean to "move from the stage of love games to the uttermost depths of crime"? Such a statement deliberately omits the crucial, intermediate stage, the stage at which the games cease to be games, at which they cease to be amusing and become encumbrances upon conscience, until eventually conscience vanishes.

Probably the world is such that play in whatever form is reassuring. Play has its ups and downs. Sometimes you win, sometimes you lose. In play passion is more or less free to slake its thirst. The game is its own safety valve. Usually the only risk is that you won't be able to stop playing, but always the same game—no surprises. Vice itself—that fixed, definitive form of play—is usually more amusing than frightening. The gentleman from Dijon, a bureaucrat, perhaps, who goes to Paris on Saturdays to take part in a skillfully staged sexual game and who returns to Dijon on Sunday to go to church, does not frighten us. To us his story is almost academic. With miraculous perspicacity he has found what his sexual tastes require (I do not accuse him, I absolutely refuse to condemn any "form of sexuality"), and he will cling to this satisfaction as tenaciously as he protects his so-

---

*I remember reading a letter written around the turn of the century by a well-known sadistic criminal. The letter proceeded normally until the criminal came to the exact moment of the murder he had committed. All at once he began using an extraordinary, unintelligible language, full of onomatopoeia but written in a beautiful handwriting. I felt that I had suddenly entered into the "reality" of the shadows to which I allude here.

cial status and family reputation. Here, however, in the infernal quest for such satisfaction, the world is suddenly turned upside down. Everything seems strange. Including the ugliness of Simone Deschamps. We cease to understand because she was ugly. Then we discover that Evenou knew she was ugly. He went so far as to denounce her ugliness in public, in the crudest of terms. He made fun of her. And she accepted both her ugliness and his mockery. Just as she accepted his disgraceful public mockery of her love for him. For she knew that he had succumbed to her ugliness, that she had become irreplaceable. And she put up with his disgusting crudeness toward her, as though it were willed by fate, as though it came from God.

Let conscience sacrifice itself sometimes, rather than take refuge in the duplicity of the so-called common morality.

"Why were you naked under the cloak? Wearing high-heel shoes and black gloves?"

"Those were the doctor's orders, your honor."

"Why weren't you wearing *normal clothing*?"

Laughter in the courtroom. With good reason. What "normal clothing" Simone Deschamps should have worn to commit her crime is not specified.

"The reason," explains Judge Bonhoure, "is that you are a monstrous sexual pervert and you were looking for unusual sensations."

The witness is reminded of the peculiar nature of her sexual relations with Evenou, of her "decadent practices," of her performance of acts of prostitution with North Africans as Evenou looked on, of her use of the whip.

"Yes, your honor," replies Simone Deschamps. "That is correct, your honor."

"Witnesses will be called tomorrow who will say that they participated in these acts," the judge threatens.

She does not answer. The case moves on. The prosecutor and the judge take the tone of severe censors. They scold the witness. She looks like a person being scolded. Stupidity fills the room, and we all participate in it. Eventually, no doubt, one becomes accustomed to such stupidity. For me it was new, suffocating, almost sickening.

"One time . . . naked . . . with two women . . . Evenou was

there . . . witnesses testified that you experienced considerable pleasure."

"Not at all, your honor."

"Then what was in it for you when you did such things?"

"I loved him, your honor."

What do these gentlemen want? The gentlemen of the court, I mean. If Simone Deschamps were to writhe on the floor in remorse, still they would not be satisfied. She admits almost all the charges, all the facts. She admits to having taken part in the most perverse acts. But they want her to admit that those acts gave her pleasure. She denies it. And for that she is admonished. Very severely. She lowers her head and does not answer. In such moments, perhaps, we glimpse unsuspected depths of servility. When she says, "I did it on the doctor's orders," that is when she is frightening. But the court says: "Some orders should not be carried out." She makes a gesture with her hand as if to say that his honor is quite right to make such a judicious observation. Only the problem is, there are people, and she is one of them, whose passion is to carry out orders.

"I Can't Explain"

What I would like to be able to describe is the psychological state of the accused in the packed courtroom on Tuesday afternoon. Her attitude was purely functional, probably rather like her attitude toward Dr. Evenou. Simone Deschamps has nothing to say, because the court forces her to say it in its language. Hence she speaks of the "atrocity" of her crime. She adopts the moral attitudes of the presiding judge in judging her own actions. And when, at the end of yesterday's session, she cried out in a low voice, "Leave me alone," she meant that she had come to the end of her silence.

I think it was the civil plaintiff's lawyer who said that Simone Deschamps's defense was rather simple-minded. In reality it was no defense at all. So that when she twice declared that she "would like to explain but I can't," no one insisted that she try. I had no idea that the accused were prevented from speaking in this way. They can speak only in answer to a question. And when they rise to open their mouths they are not allowed the time to frame their thoughts. The least important person in this case is obviously Simone Deschamps. She is henceforth defined solely in terms of her abominable crime, from her youth right up to the present. The whole judicial apparatus has lent itself to the effort of finding in her youth premonitory "signs" of the criminal to be. I beg pardon for my unfamiliarity with the courts. But this is flabbergasting. Those witnesses who take the stand to say something good about Simone Deschamps are not even thanked for their testimony. Some are scolded, reprimanded, because even when provoked they persist in not heaping opprobrium on the Simone Deschamps they once knew.

"She waited for him from four o'clock until nine o'clock in the evening," testified a woman who kept a restaurant in Choisy. "He humiliated her. She never protested. I felt sorry for her. He was more than sexually obsessed, he was mad. An actor, first and foremost. And repulsive." And so on.

The judge tries to get the witness to say that Evenou was this way because he knew Simone Deschamps. The witness says she doesn't know anything of the kind and refuses to budge. For this she is reprimanded.

"I will not explain anything," Simone Deschamps said on Sunday night.

And today, when the judge said that the moment had come for her to "excuse herself," she said, "I can no longer speak."

That is true. She can no longer speak. Don't misunderstand me. It's only the expression of a regret. We are the ones who are victims of injustice. There is injustice, in my opinion, when a criminal—even a criminal of the order of Simone Deschamps—is unable to tell us what she knows about herself. It's astonishing. The children are not allowed to speak at the dinner table. Reduced to the position of a child by the imperious court, Simone Deschamps holds her tongue. Not only is she of no interest to anyone else, she has ceased even to interest herself. She has ceased to be a person. She listens with vague curiosity to the witnesses who recount her past. But what she is most afraid of is being reprimanded by the judge and the plaintiff's attorney. Does prison seem preferable? Possibly. I have no opinion on responsibility in general or on the responsibility of Simone Deschamps in particular. Especially when the defendant is so betrayed by the judicial ritual that she can no longer find the words to express herself. I defy anyone to have an opinion about Simone Deschamps after attending her trial. Not even the defendant herself. As I watched her, I sometimes wondered if she remembered what she had done or if perhaps she was now under the spell of the court itself.

France-Observateur, 1957/1958

Interview with an Unrepentant Hoodlum

In order to call attention to a world about which people never speak, or speak only in mythical terms, a world that never ends— the world of the penitentiary, the shadow cast by our world— I felt I could not leave unpublished some of the statements, some of the answers given me by a former convict about his imprisonment.

Even though these statements and these answers may be painful to some readers in view of their moral, political, and religious convictions, I felt that this pain would be transitory and bearable compared with the pain inflicted on others in the name of those beliefs and convictions.

After rereading the interview, X, the ex-convict with whom I spoke, asked me not to disclose his identity, because his words, he felt, were "not irreverent enough. On a subject like this I should have taken a more aggressive tone."

I asked Jean-Marc Théolleyre, who followed X's trial in 1955, what he thought of this man. I give his reply verbatim:

"This trial was the first time I ever encountered in a courtroom

an accused man who accepted his role and who, rather than defer
to the courtroom routine, attempted to stand up for himself and
prove that he had just as much right to exist as the people who
were judging him. People who wind up in court are usually
broken by the time they get there. Either they try to minimize
their role or they deny their guilt. This case, though, involved a
man who accepted his responsibility and tried to show that the
courts and the society also ought to accept theirs."

Q. How long were you in prison?

A. This time it was eleven years and seven months, from November 1950 to January 1962 [sic]. The first time it was for
three years, from 1946 to 1949.

Q. You're thirty-five years old. How old were you when you
were free?

A. Twenty-three and twenty-four. I was out for eighteen
months.

Q. How did you first get involved in crime?

A. I was seventeen and a half. It was at the time Paris was
being liberated from the Germans. That was when I started
hanging out with hoodlums for the first time. And when I got
out of prison I hung out with others. That was the beginning.

Q. And when you got out this last time?

A. No, this time I haven't gone back. This time I tell myself
that after fourteen years in the slammer it's time to live a little.
I'm trying. I'm working. I started work two weeks after I got
out, thanks to some high school friends. I make 120,000 [old]
francs per months. But my hotel room costs me 30,000 a month.

Q. Is it tough?

A. Yeah. Your prison experience does you no good. It hardens
you. Ties you up in knots. Everything looks like shit, everything
seems absurd. Sometimes I ask myself if I can make it. But I
know that the next conviction will do me in altogether. My best
friends are "inside." The ones who are outside, I haven't done
anything to see them since I got out.

Lots of times when I'm working I feel like I'm doing something stupid. If I thought that things would always be like they
are now for me, I'd go back to crime.

Q. Does the boredom make you miss prison?

A. What do you think prison is like, to ask a question like that? The only thing that bores me is the kind of people I met in prison and don't want to see any more.

Q. Are you messed up for good at thirty-five with fourteen years of prison behind you?

A. Yes. I consider myself screwed because I don't see what I can do that would make me happy. People think you learn something in the slammer. You don't learn a thing. All that happens is that you lose the ability to enjoy life.

Q. Maybe when you say "if I thought things would always be like they are now for me," maybe we all feel that way, only the rest of us are used to it.

A. The minute somebody takes a risk, it means that he's less resigned to life as it is than the majority of other people—than you, for instance.

Q. Do you see any similarity between the sentence you just served and death?

A. No. The sentence I just served is worse than death. In September 1955 I got twenty years. When my petition for pardon was rejected I wanted to kill Gouriou, the psychiatrist, which for me was the same thing as suicide. Gouriou had testified against me in court, and his testimony read like an indictment. He hurt me more than anybody else. With his smooth delivery and scientific pretense he did the prosecutor's work for him. He testified that I was nasty, insolent, aggressive, and incorrigible. The reporter for *L'Aurore* summed it up: a dangerous wild animal.

Q. Do you think you got a fair trial?

A. No. I wasn't judged on the crimes I was charged with. If they've got you made for a "hood," they don't judge you on the facts but on your reputation. I was the only one who talked about the facts. And if you're the defendant, even just talking about the facts is considered outrageous. To defend yourself during the investigation and in court requires a good stubborn streak. To stand up to the judges and even to your own lawyer— who always recommends prudent silence—you've got to be unusually obstinate. I handled my own defense. Théolleyre wrote an article about me that ran under the headline "X transforms the role of the accused."

Q. Did you question witnesses yourself?

A. Yes. There were a lot of them, including eight cops. I was charged with "assault on police officers with intent to kill." It was because of the "intent to kill" that I faced the death penalty (and my lawyer tells me that three jurors voted to have me executed). But I denied any such intent, and nothing in the contradictory police statements proved that there was any. That didn't stop them from giving me twenty years, though.

Boiled down, the charge was firing a few shots when I was arrested on suspicion of possession of stolen jewels. The case in connection with which they tried to arrest me ended in dismissal. So it was only the rather animated discussion I had with the police—even though nobody was hurt and nobody was killed—that got me twenty years at hard labor (with eight years and ten months knocked off, partly for administrative reasons and partly thanks to the efforts of my family). I had fired at the ground, but the prosecutor cleverly claimed that I was trying to hit them with ricochets.

Q. If it hadn't been the police you'd had your discussion with, what sentence would you have got?

A. At worst my case would have gone to district court instead of superior court. And for an offense of that kind the maximum is two years.

Q. How long were you held prior to trial?

A. At that time a normal pretrial confinement was three or four years. Mine lasted five years. I met guys who were in for eight years prior to trial.

During those five years I learned quite a bit of criminal law. I did a crash course in the criminal code and practically memorized Brouchot's book, *Criminal Practice in the Courts and Tribunals*. I even advised one of the prosecutors, a guy named Barc, to read the book after I was up one time for contempt of court. I wrote him a letter: "I advise you to consult the book by Attorney Brouchot without delay. With diligence and assiduous attention to this work, it is not out of the question that you will one day be adequately prepared to discharge your functions as an official of the Ministry of Justice." I've noticed that many judges and lawyers don't know much about criminal law.

Q. What prisons have you been in over the past eleven years?

A. I did six years in a cell at La Santé. One year at Fresnes and Evreux. And four years at Poissy Central Prison, where I worked in the office for three years.

Q. In other words you did seven years of maximum security, sitting in your cell all day long?

A. Yes.

Q. Are there differences from one prison to the next?

A. Enormous differences. The difference between Melun Central and Clairvaux Central is the difference between night and day. Fresnes has always been considered easier than La Santé because the discipline is more relaxed—things are kind of a mess at Fresnes. The windows in the cells at Fresnes, unlike those at La Santé, open at a man's height, which makes a big difference to a convict. Unfortunately the new cell blocks at Fresnes are modeled after those at La Santé.

Q. Why unfortunately?

A. Because they're shitholes. You don't want to know any more.

Q. Is there no understanding official in the entire prison system?

A. I don't think so. If there were any they'd find something else to do. Although I remember one Communist guard—the system didn't like Communists—who everybody thought was all right.

Q. What is your predominant feeling about those fourteen years? Rage? Pain? Boredom?

A. The fear that I would die in prison. That's the worst. That's the difference between a stiff sentence and a light one. Your heavy hitters panic at the slightest illness. If you die a month after you get out, that's O.K., but not in the slammer. One guy died at Poissy from a simple abcess in his throat. His name was Antoine Moretti.

Q. What other fears?

A. You worry about something happening that will fix it so you'll never get out. I spent eleven years, you might say, on the edge of a cliff. Any self-respecting heavy hitter is in the same boat. As for the time, the days are long, sure, but when you look back it seems like the years go by quickly. You have no reference point, nothing to hang on to. Some guys prefer the winter because the days are shorter. The ones who are cold prefer the summer. That's the only difference between the seasons in prison.

Q. Do you always know when someone is to be executed?

A. No, not always. But if you're near the watchtower in La Santé, you hear the police motorcycles circling the prison at five in the morning.

Q. What was the reason for your disciplinary transfer from Evreux to Poissy?

A. I had eaten some endives that had been brought in clandestinely, and I refused to say where I got them. I was transferred to Poissy after a series of incidents.

Q. I was told that you staged several hunger strikes.

A. Right. Five in all, two of them for twenty-seven days. One was to obtain a parole. It got me nowhere. Judge A—— said, "Let him die."

Q. What was the worst thing you experienced?

A. The Henri Colin Criminal Medical Center when I was first held at Villejuif. I was there for two and a half years. I would rather be guillotined than go back there. I was eighteen when I went in. In those days the place was a dungeon. I was sent there for dementia praecox. The beans and split peas somehow miraculously cured me. There were very few lunatics in the place. They could do anything they wanted there. Shoot you up with morphine. Wrap wet sheets around your chest. Put you in a straitjacket. I'd rather not talk about Henri Colin. It was another psychiatrist who sent me there.

Q. Tell me about the cell in which you spent seven years.

A. If you touched one wall and stretched out both arms, your fingers came within ten inches of the other wall. With your feet on one wall and your hands on the other you could climb up to the ceiling. It was good exercise. The cell was twice my height in length. That was at La Santé. The window was high up on the wall. There was one bed and a table attached to the wall. A stool chained to the wall. A closet. You get used to a cell. When they change you, you're disoriented. Even if the cells are similar. Especially because of the pipes and ventilators you use to talk to other prisoners up to ten cells away. You get used to your neighbors.

Q. What do you think of us? Of me? Of other people?

A. You're a little like perverts with a taste for the picturesque.

Q. Do you see any connection between the crimes you were charged with and the sentence imposed?

A. No. The courts are disgusting, all courts. I prefer the English system of justice. There are innocent men in prison—you should tell people. I met some. People are rarely judged on the facts, as I told you before. O.K.? The courts are all dishonest. The guys who make a profession of judging other people, who understand nothing but "law and order"—you can't talk to them. You asked me what I learned in prison. If I learned anything it's the sleaziness of people like that. Probably I did cause harm to society like they say, but I don't give a damn, and I don't like the people who put me in prison because of it. People who use morality as an alibi are always pretty disgusting. For one man to judge another, they don't know what that means. I've only known one judge I could stand, and I want you to say so: the one who presided over my trial. Probably because he was a wealthy man and somebody who knew how to live. A guy who knows how to live is never a stuffed shirt. There are a couple of reporters I want you to mention too: Théolleyre of *Le Monde* and Irène Allier of *Franc-Tireur*. They were the only ones who treated me fairly. And also Arsène Lupin of the *Canard Enchaîné*, and Stéphen Hecquet.

Q. Did you think about the trial a lot?

A. Yeah, I thought about it for five years before it happened. And then for six years after that. The trial only lasted two days. But I think about it all the time. It used to be an obsession.

Q. In what sense?

A. I was angry with myself that I hadn't been more violent.

Later I had fits of rage for no particular reason. To the point where I couldn't sleep at night. But that's over now.

You have to watch your rage in prison. At Evreux a cat came into my cell one day at supper time. Sometimes he slept there. To a prisoner things like that are important. But one of the screws who had it in for me kicked the cat out one day when he brought me my supper. I ran down the gallery after him with an iron bar from the transom light. I wanted to kill him. But I couldn't catch him.

Q. Did the cat come back?

A. Yeah. At Poissy I almost always had a cat, but I worried about it, because people in prison eat cats.

Q. During the eighteen months you were out when you were twenty-three years old, did you love a woman?

A. No. It wasn't the time for me, I was too hungry for money.

Q. What relations did you have with the guards?

A. No problem there. To get on in prison you have to be proud. The nice guy takes it in the ear from the staff. You've got to be on a short fuse. Then "they" understand you and leave you alone. It's the only way to get along with the authorities. At La Santé, once you get into maximum security and you have a reputation as a tough guy, the screws leave you alone. That's their perverse side. At La Santé it's the tough guy who rates.

Q. What did you do the first day you got out?

A. It was the ninth of January. My mother was waiting for me at the gate. That afternoon I went with a woman. Doing without women is terrible in prison, maybe the toughest part of the whole thing. The woman I was with understood right away that I had just been released from the slammer, because I thought the blue bills were still worth a thousand francs. My feet hurt. I had to buy oversized shoes to walk at all during the first two months. Paris had changed a lot. The fashions, for example. The women are more beautiful than when I was young. The traffic was fantastic. It was incredible to be in the street. It's when I'm in the street that I tell myself it would be a pity to go back.

I rented a room. Two weeks later I found a job, thanks to some friends from high school.

Q. What do you want?

A. The first thing is, I want to keep my independence. I like money. But not like a businessman, only for what money can buy. Money is happiness, I'm certain of that.

Q. You're sure?

A. Yes. My other desire is to have a nice, light, airy apartment. I can't stand dark rooms any more.

Q. What was on your mind before you got out?

A. Finding work. I want you to write that down: when you

get out of the slammer, finding work is still the big worry. But anything is better than going to the social workers. What they have to offer is never suitable. Dordain, for example—the guy in the bonds case from Arras—they found him a job as a mason. He'd never done any manual labor in his life.

Q. And the work inside prison?

A. It's lousy. The working conditions are terrible. I was in charge of the print shop at Poissy. To get the machine fixed I had to wage constant warfare. A good worker can make up to 40,000 francs a month, but that's rare. In general a prisoner is doing well if he makes 10,000 a month. The sum is divided into tenths. The prisoner gets four-tenths, the government gets six. Of those four-tenths, two go into his ready account, one goes to pay his court costs, and one goes into his reserve account, up to a maximum of 15,000 francs.

Q. Can a better job be done, in your opinion, of preparing convicts to return to society?

A. Yes. But all the people involved in rehabilitation work, like prison visitors and penal reformers, are militant Christians, which means they're not worth shit. If you go to a rehabilitation center and refuse to say you feel remorse for the crimes you're supposed to have committed, your ass is grass. They never even considered sending me to one of those places.

Q. Do many people commit suicide in prison?

A. No, very few. I knew a guy who was in on a morals charge who was obsessed with suicide. He drove us bananas with it. Every night on the pipes. In the end we got fed up. We told him to go ahead and do it.

Q. Did he?

A. Yes. Some people find the work distracting. I preferred not to work. I read a book a day. When you don't work they're more likely to leave you alone, to forget about you. But a guy who has nothing put away and earns no money can't go to the canteen. He's got no choice but to work. In his *Treatise on Penal Science* Pinatel admits that they deliberately give you too little to eat so that you'll have an incentive to work, namely, so you can go to the canteen for extra food.

Q. What other subjects are discussed in the *Treatise on Penal Science?*

A. Working conditions in prison. But the regulations that

favor the convicts are never respected. The concessionaires carry weight down at the Ministry of Justice.

Ask any convict what he thinks of the Salvation Army. The Salvation Army exploits convicts more than those slavedriving concessionaires. It takes advantage of the fact that a convict has to work for a year on the outside, returning to prison every night, in order to get a parole. So the Salvation Army people generously offer their services. In ninety percent of the cases they pay an incredibly low wage, but the convict has no choice but to accept. A few years ago the daily wage was 100 [old] francs. For public relations they hand out packages to all the prisoners at Christmas (not to me, though: I always refused to accept anything from those shits), and they use that as a pretext to come in and force their foolishness down your throat: trombones, religious songs, and all that nonsense. And for that you lose your regular movie privileges.

Q. Why did you always insist on your status as a "common criminal"?

A. I knew what rights I was entitled to because of that status. That was my true status, the one I was supposed to have. No reason for me to accept any other.

Q. You always refused to submit to psychiatric examination.

A. Yes. Always. When I was in the orientation center at Fresnes, I went on a hunger strike. I insisted on being classified as a detainee, but the authorities refused to grant it on the grounds that my petition for appeal had been filed late. But I knew perfectly well that the petition had been registered. Because of that I was entitled to be treated as a detainee until the appeals court handed down its ruling.

I preferred ten years at hard labor to three years' prison combined with labor in the provinces. That's the worst you can get. They always send you to some place where there's nothing to do. I knew a guy who escaped from the place he'd been sent to. He came to Paris, he found a job, he was making a hundred thousand a month, he was happy. A cop recognized him. He got three months for violating his banning order and they revoked his parole for another eighteen months. His name was Dubourgeal—you can mention it.

Q. Did you write a lot of letters to judges?

A. Too many, to hear them tell it. As that psychiatrist, Gouriou, said at my trial, I'm not diplomatic. With those people I never knew when to keep my mouth shut.

Q. What is a hoodlum?

A. Someone who's learned to be a hoodlum. I can't define it for you. I'd have to cite a hundred examples to make you understand, before you could draw any general conclusion.

Q. What is your background? Or do you have more than one? You're both an intellectual and a hoodlum.

A. I'm a middle-class kid who went sour.

Q. Do you see any essential difference between your attitude, which is related to a certain kind of romanticism, and other attitudes related to other kinds of romanticism: the so-called rebellious attitudes?

A. In the first place, I'm not a romantic and I can't stand it when people stick that label on me. And in the second place, I don't know what you mean by "other kinds of romanticism: the so-called rebellious attitudes." So I'd prefer not to answer your question.

Q. Who are your favorite writers? And your favorite heroes?

A. My favorite writer is Marcel Aymé. My favorite hero is Le Négus in *L'Espoir* [Man's Hope, by André Malraux—Trans.].

Q. Did you know any Algerian political prisoners?

A. Yes. Emile Churon, who got fifteen years at hard labor—a Jewish Communist from Oran to whom I was very close. I'd like to know what happened to him.

.   .   .   .   .

Q. Many readers of *France-Observateur* have written to ask if you could say a little more about your experience in prison. Are you surprised by the interest your statements have aroused?

A. Not all that much. As soon as you attack the justice system and other smugly proper institutions, you're sure of achieving a certain success. It's strange: the bourgeois love that sort of thing! The wise guys explain the inconsistency by saying, "The French are by nature a seditious people." I explain it by saying, "The French are like a girl who likes to be beaten."

Q. That's begging the question. But leaving aside style and inspiration, any one of us can speak for the rest. But we can't speak for you. So tell us. Speak to us.

A. Don't get me wrong. If I tell you what I think about prison, it's not because I'm in favor of one kind of prison system over another. I am and I will always remain hostile to any form of imprisonment whatsoever. Make your choice: that's your affair, not mine. But I've heard too many eloquent preachers speak to this problem not to take this opportunity to let them know what I think. Eleven years in prison entitle me to an opinion on the subject. And my first conclusion is this: nothing will do more to improve the lot of your common criminal than the presence of a few political prisoners.

Credit to the Resistance

I'll speak plainly: if members of the resistance and collabora-tionists hadn't been imprisoned during and after the war, the penitentiary system would be just about the same as it was twenty years ago. When a bourgeois laments his woes, though, the do-gooders prick up their ears. Their good hearts go pitty-pat and it occurs to them for the first time that other people are still suffering the same ills and maybe it would be good to do something about it. So you see it's in the interest of every com-mon criminal to hope that the maximum possible number of political offenders will be imprisoned. In fact, the more respect-able they are, the more highly decorated, the better. That tells you more than all the treatises on penal science.

The facts are the facts: there's much less killing in the prisons now than there used to be, and beatings are no longer routine. A few of us had to die to get that much. And I'm not sorry for it. The ones who died saved the lives of a lot of good people. Mine, for example. If I had done time under the system in force twenty years ago, I probably would have been beaten to death.

I have no illusions. I know perfectly well that some deep thinkers are sorry we ever got rid of the old system, sorry that the good old methods aren't still in use. If they were consistent, they would argue that all criminals should be executed straight-away, mercilessly. From the social point of view that's the only logical solution. To keep a man living in terror for fifteen years and then set him free is absurd.

In fact, those in favor of a very harsh system don't care about society. They're just giving in to their natural sadism or accepting the first moral notion that comes into their heads: criminals must be severely punished.

Bébert the Cow

One guard at Poissy Central, who went by the nickname Bébert the Cow, used to speak nostalgically of the old system: "Believe me, pal, in those days the attitude around the slammer was different from what it is today. When the boys insulted each other back then, it always ended with somebody getting stabbed. Men were men in those days!" The thought pleased him, and it pleases me, the only difference between us being that I would like to see the same attitude today but without any nostalgia for the good old days.

It's a fact that the relaxation of discipline in the prisons has corrupted the majority of prisoners. By that I mean that they're more like you now than they used to be—you'll be happy to hear. Another factor that has contributed to the moral degradation of the prison population is the use of administrative pardons, which practically speaking didn't exist before the war. Nowadays the sentences handed down by the courts are heavier than they used to be. The reason is that the prosecutors are careful to let the jurors know that the sentence they decide on will not be served in full.

I still remember the prosecutor's summation at my trial, which was supposed to persuade the jury not to sentence me to a fixed term at hard labor: "I warn you against this final option, because a sentence of twenty years at hard labor can be considerably reduced in a variety of ways, and this defendant deserves to be put away for keeps." Needless to say, I have a particularly warm spot in my heart for that man.

The administrative pardon works like this: if a convict behaves himself all year, the warden will recommend that time be taken off his sentence for good behavior. Every Bastille Day the list of reductions is handed down. The moral effects of the system are deplorable. It's in the prisoner's interest to curry favor with the authorities. It doesn't take much imagination to see where that leads.

Socially, though, the results are excellent, at least in the majority of cases. There's no better way to mold a man's character. Hypocrisy flourishes, and the act that is put on for the benefit of the prison visitors, social workers, priests, and preachers is enough to turn your stomach. You should congratulate yourselves, of course. That's what society wants, and your representatives, the rehabilitation experts, think the system works pretty well. All their favors go to the spineless bunch who play the game. The only flaw in the system is that the job is only half done. It's not enough to get men to act like buggers' boys. You've got to accomplish something.

A Religious Conception

The only result they've obtained so far is to get guys to behave in prison the way they want them to. The underlying idea is that a criminal is not likely to find a place in society unless he is bitterly sorry for having committed the crime for which he was imprisoned. At bottom it's a religious idea, which may work in the confessional but socially speaking is no good at all.

I know what I'm talking about: remorse does not exist.

I've never met a criminal who was sincerely sorry for his crimes. Forcing a man to play-act doesn't accomplish anything. If your rehabilitation experts worried less about morality and sincerely tried to help criminals find their way back into society, the results would be a lot better.

People will accuse me of exaggerating and of twisting the facts in my own twisted mind. But I am the material that those people have to work with, and my reactions are a sounder basis for theorizing than anything those holy rollers have come up with.

The Dangers of Plain Speaking

Take my case as an example. I got bad marks throughout my incarceration. Ourcq, head of prisons for the Paris area, said that I was a typical incorrigible. He said that because my relations with the prison authorities were always strained. That's the basis on which they judge your chances for success on the outside. A man who speaks plainly and doesn't kiss ass is invariably branded a rotten apple. So, paradoxically, the prisoners considered most dangerous to society are precisely the ones for whom nothing is done.

I was twenty-four when I was arrested and twenty-nine when I was sentenced to twenty years' hard labor. Shortly after my trial I was visited by a fellow named Charels, president of the Friends of Penal Reform, who explained that he wanted to see me because of my attitude in court. What he was saying struck me as sympathetic at first, because my attitude in court had caused a scandal. He spoke warmly of the Melun Central Prison, a model of penal reform, and expressed the hope that I could serve my time there. He told me that I had made an excellent impression on him and asked me to write.

In my letter I told him, honestly, that the supervised recreational activities at Melun, of which he had spoken so enthusiastically, struck me as being a little too much like the Boy Scouts and would probably get on my nerves, but that I figured I had a better chance of getting out if I went to Melun than if I went somewhere else. That was a serious mistake. That wasn't what he expected at all. I understood that from his answer to my letter, which I cite verbatim:

31 October 1955

Sir:

I thank you for your letter and especially for the candid expression of your thoughts, which I take as license to be equally candid in my reply.

If all prisoners felt as you do, obviously I would not have spent fifteen years of my life seeking to improve prison life.

For some years now, I have been convinced that most convicts were unaware of their true nature and had no desire to escape from a way of life that they had either chosen for themselves or had thrust upon them by their early upbringing and education.

I believed that by providing prisoners with work on the one hand and worthy recreational activities on the other it might be possible to create an atmosphere more conducive to rehabilitation than by subjecting convicts to a sordid, debasing existence. That is why I fought for my ideas and often succeeded in persuading the prison authorities to adopt them. In other words, I believed that, once sentence was pronounced, it was essential to win the respect of the prisoner and make prison a useful place. I have stated my view frankly: before release can be discussed, the prisoner must transform himself in preparation for that release. Release should not mean merely unlocking the gates but true

liberation, true freedom, which involves membership in a human community, working both for oneself and for the community. It means
being respectful of the freedom of others, and, by so doing [sic], becoming free oneself.

Freedom is not a kind of anarchy, an anarchy as harmful to oneself as
it is to others.

Let me sum up your case. You are twenty-nine years old. For the
past five years you have been in a cell at La Santé. You first claimed
your "freedom" when you were eighteen years old, I believe. Not a
very distinguished career—and I am not speaking here as a moralist.
You are very intelligent, and with your intelligence, especially in view
of the support of your family, you should one day be able to do something more with your life than spend the majority of your days in
prison. But for the time being you are in prison. Will you win the parole you count on? That is not up to me. But consider two possibilities:

1. Your sentence is reduced immediately to ten years.

2. You stay at twenty years.

Case 1: You have only five years left to serve, and you think you
might be assigned an outside job, selling hot dogs, say, in Mulhouse. I
choose this example because you say you were told that at Mulhouse
the convicts work outside the prison. In both Mulhouse and Melun,
the new penal system is in force. Under this system you must spend
one year in a cell under observation to determine what category you
belong in: 1) capable of rehabilitation, 2) doubtful, or 3) incorrigible.

In the second year you work in a group. If you were in category 3,
you can rise to category 1 or 2. If you were in category 1, you can be
demoted to category 2 or 3.

In the third year, if you were in category 1, you may be promoted to
the outstanding category (meritorious prisoners).

In the fourth year, you are eligible for work release if you are in the
top category.

Case 2: In theory you have fifteen years left. The procedure is the
same at Mulhouse, Caen, or Melun, except that only prisoners with
three or four years' time remaining are eligible for work release. Before
you're sent to one of the central prisons, you go to Fresnes for observation. There, specialists will determine where you should be sent: to
one of the three reformed central prisons, or to another central prison,
not yet reformed, where you have been told that the situation is one
"God-awful mess," though I doubt this is the case.

The truth is I can't give you any advice. You will act in accordance
with your desires for the future. I cannot say that if you go to Melun,
everything possible will be done to get your sentence reduced. It
would be misleading to tell you that. What I can say is that in a prison

like Melun, which I know best, a man who wants to make a moral recovery can find all the help he needs. He will find it with the warden, with the prison teachers, with the prison visitors, and with the artists, whose attitude is not that of Boy Scouts and not patronizing.

But my sense of you, as you showed yourself during my visit and in your letter, makes me uncertain whether you would thrive in such a climate.

You are not a man who understands that he has taken a wrong turn in life but one who is still fighting solely to get out of prison. No doubt I seem to be taking your plight very lightly. But no, I assure you that I understand or at any rate that I am trying to understand.

Best wishes,
Charels

Cops

Sickening style aside, the letter, you've got to admit, is nothing but a sermon. I cited it at length because I think it's significant. Some of your readers will no doubt find it on the whole quite reasonable, but that's because the letter implies that in my interview with this guy I said things that led him to believe I couldn't wait to get back to robbing banks or mugging the elderly the minute I got out. I'm not that stupid. To me people like him are cops, pure and simple. I didn't trust him.

When he broached the subject of my future and my plans, I told him in a very sincere tone that I was firmly resolved to resume a normal life, that I didn't want to die in prison, and that I understood that it was in my interest to change my ways if I wanted to live a little. What else did that bird want? He didn't feel in his little soul that my heart had been engulfed by holy fire. He wanted me to say I was sorry. He probably thought that my desire to get out of prison as quickly as possible was inappropriate.

As far as he's concerned, the first thing a prisoner has to do is expiate his crime, start down the road to moral recovery. That phrase, "moral recovery," stuck in my throat. I sent the guy a letter and told him, admittedly in not very polite terms, where to get off. But the prejudice is very firmly rooted, so you'll probably tell me I was in the wrong and this fellow Charels was defending society as he should.

When the champions of penal reform understand that you can't change a man's attitude but you can induce a criminal to change his way of life by offering him the opportunity to live decently without breaking the law, then and only then will they do useful work. Nothing worthwhile has been done up to now, I can tell you that. True, there's a print shop at Melun where convicts in for long terms can learn the printing trade. But that's an exception in the French prison system. What is more, that print shop existed before there was any thought of penal reform, and the only reason it's there is that the bureaucracy found it advantageous to run its own printing plant. Convict labor, woefully underpaid, is useful, and government documents are printed in the prison at low cost.

The convicts at Melun take their revenge in their own way. I heard from a clerk in the records office at Poissy that nobody there ever licks an envelope printed at Melun. They use a sponge, because the prisoners at Melun piss in the glue. I imagine that this news will provoke outrage in government offices all over France. Anyway, the point is that one print shop can't solve the problems of all the prisoners in the country.

Contrary to the expectations of all officials, I've been working since I got out of prison, but let me assure you that the climate I lived in during my eleven years on the inside in no way contributed to my decision.

No Choice for Hoodlums

Rehabilitation is aimed mainly at those prisoners with heavy sentences. Now, rehabilitation is of no use to those in on morals charges, because most of them led normal social lives before they were arrested. The petty criminals, the crooks who come back to prison regularly, also worked for the most part. It's because they worked and got sick of it that they went back to crime. So penal reform really affects only those guys who deliberately chose to lead lives in which work played no part at all. I maintain that many hoodlums who have served long sentences feel, even if they won't admit it, a kind of fatigue, a fear of going back to the kind of life they had led before going to prison. They've wasted ten years of their lives in prison, and they know better than anyone else the uncertainties of the criminal life. Their friends from before have often let them down. Their experience in prison makes them more afraid than ever of being arrested again, and they're only too well aware of their vulnerability.

But they have no choice. You don't give them any choice. When they get out, the only people they can count on are other criminals, and that's not where they're likely to find regular and legitimate work.

Going to one of the official prisoners' aid agencies—if you know what that means, you know that going there does about as much good as dropping your drawers. Obviously all you "straights" will think that if only these guys had enough "courage" they would do whatever they had to do to stay "honest." You're like dogs on a leash, and with your romanticism you'd like to see them sign up for the Foreign Legion to redeem their crimes (and you probably don't even know that common criminals aren't allowed to join the legion).

There's only one thing that you'll never get through your little heads: these guys don't suffer from a bad conscience, and if they had to express their feelings toward you with a single gesture, they'd spit in your face. When I say that many of these men are capable of rehabilitation and of living in your society, I mean that they're in the same boat as me: they don't want to go back to prison, and you folks are too good at protecting your dough.

Your Lovely Dough

But that doesn't make them candidates for sainthood.

If they aren't lucky enough to know people who can get them a suitable job, then they have no option but to try their luck. And I say more power to them.

The majority of you will probably say that it is not desirable to do anything for men who harbor such sentiments toward society. That, in fact, is the attitude of prison officials. Think what you like. Refuse to solve a social problem because you find it shocking to help rehabilitate men who detest you. But don't be surprised if they bare their teeth. Don't complain if some day one of them asks you, not too politely, to hand over your lovely dough. And if by chance you get shot in the face, I personally will be delighted.

I'll be particularly delighted if you work for a bank for 80,000 a month and kick up a fuss trying to save the bank's dough. To me, that bank clerk symbolizes all that is most hateful, but to you he's probably pleasant and reassuring. He doesn't ask any questions, he knows the difference between right and wrong at all times, he knows the law. He'll also make a fine juror, capable of judging as severely as one might wish the recidivist who hasn't had the "courage" to find honest work.

It's just like you, it's all made in your image, in the image of your kind of society: a society in which the most cowardly of men can play at being a big cheese, as long as he's backed up by some organized institution.

France-Observateur, 1957

The Two Ghettos

Marguerite Duras first interviewed two Algerian workers living in
Paris, X and Z (for obvious reasons we cannot reveal their identity) and
then interviewed a young survivor of the Warsaw ghetto, M (who did
not want her name to be used). Similar questions were put to all three
people. Here are their answers.

Q. Do you live in fear all the time, or are there moments
when you feel less afraid?
A. X: I am always afraid of dying. When an Algerian leaves for
work, he asks himself, Will I come home tonight? He is afraid
on his way to work and on his way back. After he puts on his
work uniform and is on the job, he is a little less afraid. I live in
a hotel where all the clients are Algerian. At night, when there's
a noise on the stairway, we all wake up and we wait. The thought
goes through our minds that we're about to be killed. When you,
a French person, see a policeman with a submachine gun, you're
afraid, too—of the submachine gun—but we're afraid that he's
actually going to fire a burst. We're afraid, sure, but by now the

117

fear is inside us, it's part of us. It's a shadow that's always with us. Like when a man walks and his shadow follows along behind, that's what our fear is like.

A. Z: I'm afraid. I have nothing on me. I'm afraid anyway. It's risky even to stop at a cafe for a drink. It's risky to buy shoes. Two weeks ago I went to buy shoes on the boulevard Saint-Michel. It was three o'clock in the afternoon. I was arrested and taken to the station house, and they held me there for two days. You can't go from one part of Paris to another. Ten minutes on the Metro is too long. I haven't heard from my cousin, who lives in the Nineteenth Arrondissement, since the demonstrations. I live in the Fifth Arrondisement. . It's impossible for me to get out there. *I am afraid of being Algerian.* When I see the police, I cross the street. But once they've arrested me I stop being afraid. Before being arrested I think of my wife, I think of my children, and I'm afraid. Afterward I stop.

Fear

Q. Are there ways to reduce your fear? I mean, to minimize your risks?

A. Z: I don't wear a scarf or a tie. That way they can't strangle me. You can't wear a tie or a watch or a wedding ring when you go out. We all take these precautions now.

Q. Your fear is of the unknown. You never know why or how danger may strike.

A. X: Never. On the day of the strike I went to the movies. At two in the afternoon I was arrested, taken to the police station, and beaten. I don't know why. Yesterday a friend of mine was arrested and beaten—he's been asleep for twenty-four hours. He doesn't know why he was arrested. It's just something that comes over them [i.e., the police—trans.]. They stole 50,000 francs of savings from one pal of mine, 10,000 francs from another, 300 francs from another—all they had. They tear up our pay vouchers and our residence permits. They do these things whenever they please. In the police stations there's one guy with a hammer. They say, "Hold out your left hand." They take our watches, and the guy with the hammer smashes them and throws them into a pile of smashed watches. Why? We never know when or why.

Q. Why do they beat you and kill you, in your opinion? Are they afraid of you?

A. X: I don't think so. It's hatred. Remember, Arabs have always been insulted, always. But as long as they were inoffensive, as long as they were just picturesque visitors in the streets, it didn't go beyond insults. It's only since the Arab has begun to hold his head high, to be something more than a beast of burden, to demand his dignity, that things have gotten worse. That's when the beatings started.

A. Z: It's hatred, for sure.

A. X: We are constantly afraid of being killed. Now that the curfew is later, we're even more afraid. The change in the curfew was a defeat for the police, so we're even more afraid.

A. X: We've got to stick together. Our only protection is to go where there are lots of people. On Saturdays and Sundays, for example, the best place for us to go is the Grands Boulevards. Even if only ten percent of the crowd is on our side, it keeps them from trying anything. The main thing is not to find yourself alone with them on a deserted street. If that happens you know you're going to wind up either in a police station or in the Seine.

A. Z: Yes, it's better to tangle with them with people around than when you're all alone. But on my days off I've taken to staying home. I don't dare go out. I read the newspapers. I'm afraid of the dogs at Vincennes and the Porte de Versailles.

Q. What about lodging?

A. Z: It's still easy to find a room, but you have to be careful. It's the same story. The worst thing for us would be to live among you. We've got to band together. We can live only in a group. If I were the only Algerian in a hotel full of French, I'd be arrested the day after I moved in. If you live in a group, you hear news of those who are arrested by the cops.

Q. Food?

A. X: More terror. You go to a restaurant, say. You barely have time to put in your order before the police arrive. Everybody is arrested. In the street they dump out our bowls and then they say, "That's shit, boy. Pick it up off the ground." That happens all the time. If you don't pick it up, they club you.

Happiness

Q. Do you still have an uncomplicated, simple idea of happiness?

A. X: Yes. I pray to God that I live until independence. If I can see my flag flying over my homeland, I don't care what happens after that. As long as I've been alive it's the French flag that I've seen flying in my country. In France, too, I see the French flag all the time.

A. Z: For me, happiness is an end to all this hatred. No more fear, no more terror. All I want is to go out in the street without anybody giving me angry looks. I want to walk down streets that the cops don't own.

Q. Do you still have hopes for yourself personally? Personal plans?

A. X: Not for the time being. The only desire in the hearts and minds of all Algerians is to see the Algerian flag flying over their country. It's hard to find an Algerian who will tell you, "I want something, a car and maybe a suit." We've lost our appetite for such things. Even for clothes. I haven't shaved for three days. It's been three months since I've been to a barber. Friends of mine cut their hair very short so they don't have to bother about it any more.

A. Z: I'd like to send some money to my wife. The rest I'll spend. I'm completely discouraged. We're like zombies.

Q. Love, in France, for an Algerian—what does that mean?

A. X: For women, in the past, there was still hope. Not anymore. They're afraid, too. A French woman who is with an Algerian is in for a rough time herself. For us to be loved by a French woman is out of the question. The French women who might have gone with us go with the blacks instead. There are the prostitutes. But we've lost our appetite even for prostitutes. For an Algerian man in France the game is up; love is a figment of his imagination.

A. Z: In the Sixth Arrondissement you can still approach a woman, but not anywhere else.

Q. Do you think your situation is similar to anyone else's, and if so, whose?

A. X: I think of the Hindus before Indian national independence, even before Gandhi. Friends of mine say we're like the Jews under the German occupation. They say, "It's just like Eichmann's day. The only thing that's missing is the crematories and the gas chambers."

Q. In these terrible circumstances what rights do you still have?

A. X: (Laughs.) We have insurance. We have the right to file a complaint. The friend of mine from whom the cops stole 50,000 francs asked how to file a complaint. He was told to go to a police station. A month ago a friend of mine was arrested. A cop kicked him in the head and he lost an eye. He hasn't been seen since. I'm sure the cops took him out in the woods somewhere and killed him because he was too badly injured to release. And if his body is found, they'll say it was just some Algerians settling scores among themselves. What right do I have to find out what happened? If I try to find out, I'll wind up in jail.

Q. And your loneliness? Your boredom?

A. X: I feel lonely. I am lonely in a way no European can imagine or understand, far from my home and my family. Fortunately there are a lot of us. You people have no idea of the solidarity that there is among us. Through hunger, solitude, and mistreatment we are all brothers. You have no idea of that. We look forward to only one thing: going home.

A. Z: I don't know what to do anymore when I'm not working. I'm horribly bored. We live and work against our will. I'm completely discouraged.

Work

Q. What about work?

A. X: I've been fired from my job, along with three of my friends. No hope for us there either. We miss too many days of work. We're arrested too often. We give our employers headaches.

A. Z: I have a good boss. I'm still working. I'm a cook and work nights, and when my night travel permit was torn up, my boss got me a new one. At work I'm happy. Outside of work it's terrible. At night you're good or bad depending on their whims. If you're an Algerian, nobody ever asks who you are.

Q. What do you think of the French workers' attitude toward you?

A. X: You have to say that French workers don't treat us very fairly. If we're on an equal level with them, it's O.K. But if we have some skill, if we make more per hour, it's not O.K. at all. It's the same for Italian, Portuguese, and Spanish workers, but they're more jealous of us than of any of the others. It's inevitable—we know that.

Q. How do you see us? All alike?

A. X: No, we don't hate all the French. Even among cops there are differences. Once I heard a cop tell another cop to stop beating somebody. Another time a sergeant at the station house released me because he said he knew me by sight, we were neighbors.

A. Z: Sure, we know that some French people are on our side.

Q. How would you compare the life you lead to the life that French people in general lead?

A. X: The life the French lead seems like a miracle to us. Even a worker in France lives like a pasha.

Q. What words define your life?

A. X: Terrorized: That says it all. We lead a terrorized life. We are despised, deprived of our honor and dignity—in the eyes of our bosses and even of many French workers. You can't imagine what it's like—nobody in France can. That's a big difference. You ask me for a word: It's racism. That's the big difference between you and me, THAT WORD. Many French people look at us and see the devil. We know that. Many French people would take the law into their own hands, if they could. We know that, too. We see them looking at us, and we know what those looks mean. When we take the Metro home from work and discover that we're the only Algerian in the car, we know that we're the plague incarnate. A few days ago I found myself in that situation: the only Algerian in a subway car. Among the French people in the car was an old woman who was standing quite close to me, her handbag rubbing up against me. Next to her were two policemen. So I did what we always do in such situations: I put both hands in my belt, over my stomach, in plain view, and I turned around.

The old woman also turned and moved back in front of me. She did it twice. I was afraid. I shoved people without excusing myself. A seat was open and I took it. The old woman wound up next to me again. Everybody was looking at us. But at the other end of the car there was another old woman who intervened. She said to the first woman, "I'm watching you. What you're doing is an injustice." When I'm the only Algerian in a place, I know, I feel, that I'm the devil in person.

A. Z: I no longer have the right to have an argument with another man. Any Frenchman who differs with me is in the right, no matter what the circumstances. I always have to back down. I'm helpless.

Vengeance

Q. The police station? The Seine?

A. X: In this one police station there's a cellar. Unfortunately you'll never see it.

We all think about the Seine. Many of us come from mountain villages and don't know how to swim.

Q. Vengeance?

A. X: If the FLN [Algerian National Liberation Front] orders us to attack the police, afraid or not, unarmed or not, not many would hesitate to carry out the order, I assure you. But the FLN won't give such an order. We're not even allowed to carry nail files in our pockets. When the cops search us every night in our hotels, they know that. One of the reasons they're so angry is that they never even find a nail file on us.

Interview with M, Survivor of the Warsaw Ghetto

Q. Did you live in fear all the time, or were there moments when you felt less afraid?

A. I was very small. We were afraid of dying of hunger. But until the uprising we were not especially afraid. We were afraid of the armed Germans who came into the ghetto, and we were afraid of running into a German, but those were passing fears. We were much safer in the ghetto, among ourselves, than we were outside. My father was assimilated and could have hidden with Aryans he knew, but he always came back to the ghetto. He even refused the offer of one German to hide him in Germany. It wasn't just solidarity that kept him in the ghetto, it was the feeling of security. I was very small, but I felt humiliated that I was imprisoned in the ghetto, defenseless. They succeeded in making me feel that way.

Fear

Until the uprising there were ways of warding off the fear. Just to stay alive at all costs was in itself a defense against fear. When the uprising came, many Jews committed suicide. At that point suicide became the equivalent of what the effort to stay alive had been before the uprising; it was a way of defending ourselves against the death that the Germans had in store for us. To kill oneself seemed preferable. During the uprising, from July to November 1942, the fear took a definite form: that of death. At that point, I remember, I was afraid all the time. The Germans were constantly in the ghetto. Each day they shrank the ghetto a little bit more, and each day we felt the presence of death a little more strongly.

Q. You were telling me that you were eight years old when a German policeman took a shot at you because you tried to flee the room when he entered. What was that German like?

A. He was very calm. In the ghetto, even when they slapped us, even when they shot at us, they remained impassive. When I think of the Germans in the ghetto, I think of calm, cold men. They spoke to us familiarly. They called us "dirty Jews." But I remember that in 1940 one German addressed my grandmother as "Madame." Not after that, though. In the camps they were awful to the deportees, because they lived with them in the same place. In the camps the life of the S.S. was linked to that of the Jews. In the ghetto they came as visitors, they did their killing, and they went back to Warsaw for lunch.

Q. Tell me about the problems of housing and food.

A. I never went hungry. My family was wealthy. Contraband food was very expensive, but my parents could afford to buy it. On my way to class, though, I saw bodies, mostly of young children. My first teacher died of hunger. The housing problem was terrible. The provincial ghettos had been moved lock, stock, and barrel into Warsaw, so the problem of housing assumed tragic proportions. People lived in the streets and died in the streets. There was no public transportation.

Happiness

Q. Did you still have an uncomplicated, simple idea of happiness?

A. Happiness was pre-war. A normal life, even with anti-Semitism, was happiness.

Q. Did you still have hopes for yourself personally? Personal plans?

A. The main concern of every Jew in the ghetto was to survive the ghetto. During the uprising we thought we would all die. Before that it was possible to entertain personal hopes. I remember that my mother occasionally had a dress made. During the uprising, of course, personal plans were out of the question.

Q. Love, in the ghetto—what did that mean?

A. Love, along with every other form of life, existed in the ghetto. Love in the ghetto saved some people and lost others—couples who refused to separate. I do not believe that there was such a thing as love between Germans and Jews in the ghetto. Jewish girls who left the ghetto and were picked up in Warsaw were brought back to the ghetto and shot.

Q. Did you think your situation was similar to anyone else's, and if so, whose?

A. No one's. But if you're asking whether I think it is still possible for a ghetto to exist, the answer is yes. I believe that there are always "objective" conditions that can assume this form. The Algerian business is horrible, but it has not assumed this form. If the French police are hypersensitive to the Algerians, they're no different, I think, from the police in any of the countries that are threatened with or in the process of losing their colonies. I found out yesterday that many Algerians have been found drowned in the Seine. That doesn't surprise me. It's almost in the natural order of things. Politically, I can't get excited about anything anymore, and nothing surprises me.

Q. In the terrible circumstances of the ghetto what rights did you still have?

A. We had the Judenrat [or Jewish Council, the ghetto's internal governing body—Trans.]. A Jew who robbed another Jew was punished. A German who robbed a Jew was never punished. A Jew who robbed a German would have been shot.

Work

Q. What about work?

A. My father, who was a chemist, worked very hard. My mother, a bacteriologist, also worked very hard. Work was very important, a moral as well as a physical defense. A person without work was likely to die of hunger and, worse still, in humiliation.

Q. How did you see the Germans? All alike?

A. To me they were all alike. But even in the ghetto my father was visited by a German friend. That German was shot in 1944.

Q. What words defined your life?

A. I don't know. That's a difficult question. Some people say, "I'm happy to have survived such an experience, because it enriched my life morally." To me such an attitude is revolting. I mean that, given all the people who died, to find the ghetto experience interesting is something that revolts me. The ghetto is utterly revolting to me. I understand the Algerians' point of view. They are a nation. We were not a nation. Suppose, for example, you took all the small businessmen in France and locked them up in a ghetto. What would they do? That was the way it was with the Jews. The Algerians are a people.

Vengeance

Q. Vengeance?

A. I was too little, I had an inferiority complex toward Germans. But my father often said, "When the Russians get here, I'll join the N.K.V.D. [the Russian secret police before the K.G.B.—Trans.] and kill them all."

France-Observateur, 1961

Dialogue with a Carmelite

Our purpose here is to relate an experience honestly lived and honestly transcended. Unless we are willing to limit our role as purveyors of information, we cannot refuse to relate one kind of experience because we would rather talk about another. There is no special audience for this kind of truth. Truth is not aristocratic or exclusive but belongs to everyone, and the most homely item of local news is as unfathomable as anything that happens anywhere in the province of heart and mind. Heart and mind, we believe, are the world's most widely shared possessions, and even though we expect to be attacked in any number of contradictory ways for printing this story, we think it our duty to do so.

Q. Do you think that the "truth" about the Carmelite convent in which you lived for fifteen months is of such a special kind that not everyone will be able to understand it?

A. I don't think so. Anyone who is open to an honest account of a sincere experience will agree, I think, and will not claim to understand more than can be understood.

Q. Are published accounts of the Carmelite life true or false?

A. It's not that they're false, just that they're as far from the truth as my own ideas about the life before I entered the convent. The difference is just as great. You imagine a kind of moving picture of a life in which people pad around silently and peace reigns in the cloister. But that picture is false.

Q. In other words, the Carmelite life is very different from what one would expect.

A. Yes. It is impossible to imagine in advance what the life is actually like. But there is nothing shocking in that, since a person enters a convent only after deciding to give up everything human. Everything in the convent is opposed to nature, but that one expected. That is not the problem. The problem is whether or not one can endure such a life. And generally one can. Nature is clever. It adapts, it compensates in all sorts of ways.

Q. For example?

A. For example, with laughter: within a half hour of entering the convent I was horrified by the laughter. It was twelve-thirty in the afternoon, recreation time, in the middle of spring. I wanted to leave immediately. The mistress of novices and twenty Carmelites were laughing raucously. I wondered what they could be laughing about in a Carmelite convent. It was horrifying. You enter the convent with an idea of the absolute. You expect to find a very serious, mystical atmosphere. And instead you find twenty nuns laughing their heads off.

Q. About what?

A. About everything. About nothing. Seldom in my life have I found it possible to laugh. They laugh because a chick is born black rather than yellow. Or because someone spilled some soap. They laugh over trifles. That's what I meant when I said that nature adapts, that nature is very clever. Broadly speaking, the nuns considered to be good nuns are happy nuns.

Q. Are the two hours of recreation period the only time that the Carmelites are allowed to talk among themselves?

A. Yes. The constant silence is also very hard on the nerves. But it is busy silence, mind you. Nuns work. They mend linen. They rebind books and missals, sometimes works by [Paul] Claudel and [Charles] Péguy. They make hosts, reliquaries, and holy images. But reading is out of the question, except for religious books. It's a frightful intellectual vacuum.

Q. Leaving aside the aspects of conventual life that everyone knows about, can you tell me what is hardest to bear?

A. Everything is hard. You sleep only six hours per night, professed nuns and novices alike. During morning prayers some of the nuns fall asleep on their knees as they sway back and forth. The dress is also hard to take. It's the same the year round: a used frock in summer, a new frock in winter, with a tunic of white wool underneath. After six months, when you're no longer a postulant, they take away all your underwear. Winter and summer you're naked under your frock. For washing you have only one pitcher of cold water each day, and once a week a large jug of hot water. You have to make do, and people do. You used to have to wear a white wool gown while washing. Everything is hard, except the work.

Q. Doesn't the work compensate for the constant silence?

A. Not entirely. The work is a physical occupation that leaves the mind free. It's supposed to be done, moreover, in a prayerful frame of mind. But when you have a complicated job to do, you feel relatively happy.

Q. Can you tell me something about the two-hour recreation period during which the rule of silence is suspended?

A. The triviality of the conversations is astonishing. Since all personal conversation is supposedly forbidden, as is any allusion to one's past, the Carmelites gossip like housewives. I think that women suffer more than men from the rule of silence.

Q. What you're telling me is terrifying. Is that the wrong word to use?

A. No, that's the right word. One feels panic, vertigo, at discovering this void. Fortunately, you're not always aware of it. One takes an enormous risk gambling one's life on an absolute of this sort. The proportions of failure are so great that the mere prospect is terrifying.

Q. Is there any kind of private life or society that develops in spite of the community's taboos? Can one speak of a society?

A. Yes.

Q. In what sense?

A. In relations between the nuns and their superiors. In the nuns' work relations. In their mute interactions, their gestures. Of twenty nuns, three or four effectively manage not to have any social relations with the other sisters. Some don't even have to fight the temptation, but such cases are quite rare. A society is born, in fact, when a nun finds it more pleasant to meet one of her sisters in the corridors rather than another.

Q. Do you think that the physical hardships you mentioned a moment ago, by themselves, can destroy a person's faith?

A. No, because those hardships have always been there and are equally difficult for everyone—the older nuns speak warmly of their initial difficulties, of the enormous appetites they used to have, and so on. In any case, the hardships are an intrinsic part of the faith. One comes looking for hardships to face, even if one is surprised by what turns out, in fact, to be most difficult. And then there are ways of releasing the tension, outlets for the rage that one feels at not being able to put up serenely with the difficulties.

Q. Corporal penances?

A. Yes. Twice a week the nuns "discipline themselves." It's done in a group in the chapel choir. Frocks pulled up to the waist, the sisters flagellate themselves with scourges of plaited rope. All the lights are extinguished and black curtains are drawn, and everyone recites the Miserere. Although this act is in theory a penance, that is, a positive act of love of God and renunciation of oneself, it is also, in fact, a necessary physical outlet, a way of expressing the rage that one feels against oneself.

Q. Is there a sexual component? You are free not to answer, of course.

A. I will answer. Yes. There is, quite simply, a necessary sexual component, although most nuns are certainly unaware of it.

Q. You said earlier that nature is very clever. Would you say that it is even more clever in its sexual aspect?

A. Man is forgotten. But despite the impersonality of the relations, it is undeniable that in every convent certain nuns exert almost amorous powers of attraction on others.

Q. Can one speak of love?

A. Probably. By way of shrewd compensations, more or less consciously adopted.

Q. Let's get back to penances. Is there not a danger that progress in psychology and psychoanalysis will change our understanding of the meaning of penance?

A. Yes. Especially since Saint John of the Cross and Saint Teresa of Avila warned against the "self-seeking" involved in excessive penance. This is the reason for the prohibition against practicing certain kinds of penance without the approval of one's superiors. The mistress of novices reminds you of this rule about a month after you enter the convent, when she instructs you in the "discipline" of the establishment. The reminder is also couched in indirect language. From then on the subject is never again mentioned.

Q. Are there voluntary as well as compulsory penances?

A. Yes. There are iron bracelets with claws that you put around your arm. Nobody forces you to, however—absolutely nobody. The goal is not suffering but the exercise of willpower; you fight against any tendency toward self-indulgence.

Q. Now that you have some distance on it all, do you think that these exercises of the will were absurd or not?

A. No. They may seem absurd to you, because these ascetic practices have no equivalent in ordinary life. But they produce extraordinary results. They help to keep nuns balanced and lucid and to teach them about the nature of man by teaching them about themselvs; they also teach the nun about the infinitely many ways in which God can be loved. Nuns are exceptional people. The will to prayer is not an idle phrase. These practices may shock you, but they are in the tradition of the Desert Fathers, the eastern tradition, and very common in the contemplative orders.

Q. You see nothing in lay life even remotely equivalent to this kind of experience?

A. Religiously speaking, people who have the faith would answer you by saying that in ordinary life, in society, the love of God can be achieved through equal fervor in prayer, though much more rarely than in the convent. The reason is that the cloister is organized expressly for the contemplation of God; with all human distractions and interests eliminated, it is the ideal place to achieve a perfect love of God. Humanly speaking, I don't feel that the constraints of prison are comparable. I will say this though, based on personal knowledge—I was held for several weeks once as a political prisoner: since one goes to prison against one's will, prison is an even more perfect renunciation of personal will than is the voluntary decision to enter a convent. In a Carmelite convent you are among peers. In the eyes of God you are nothing, but that nothingness leaves your dignity intact. What is more, you have the sense of an exceptional vocation. You don't go to prison with the same degree of self-esteem with which you enter a convent. Or at least few people do. Though come to think of it, the writings of Jean Genet remind me of those of Saint John of the Cross. Genet's experience of abjection is of a mystical order because he doesn't avert his eyes, and finds salvation and dignity in rebellion.

Q. Does prison provide its own outlets for rage?

A. Of course: rebellion. That rebellion has no limits, since one's jailer is by definition contemptible, even if he is not personally a bastard.

Q. Is the opportunity for what you call unlimited rebellion one of the "attractions" of prison?

A. Yes. It's also a gift. I have seen delinquents on whom prison exerted a kind of fascination, much like the fascination that the convent exerts on certain Carmelites, especially the simpler girls. Because, you know, there are nuns who claim to have endured twenty years of darkest night when in fact they've simply spent twenty years in a vacuum.

Q. Is it difficult to become a Carmelite?

A. Yes. Not just anyone can enter the convent. Vocations are reviewed. In principle a dowry is required, especially to become a "choir nun." * Only applicants judged superior are admitted without a dowry. Certain convents are wealthy, others poor; this raises a variety of problems. The resources of a small, cloistered community living in accordance with a centuries-old model are limited. With that we come to the thorny problem of money and the Church. The Church is an established power: that is its strength, but it is also the reason for its sterility.

Q. Can religious communities be viewed as democratic?

* There are four kinds of Carmelite nuns: the superior prioress, the professed nuns, the lay sisters, and the extern sisters.

A. No, they are the opposite of democratic. The lay sisters are like the convent's servants. They do the heavy work. They do not attend services (although they recite the rosary a good deal) and spend much less time in the choir. They have, quite literally, no "voice" in the chapter. In other words, when the nuns begin deliberating matters concerning the material and spiritual welfare, the lay sisters are asked to leave the meeting. Although lay sisters, it is generally acknowledged, can be as mystical and holy as choir nuns, they are in a social sense second-class citizens. They must suffer from this.

Q. When a person becomes aware of her singularity—in this case, her vocation—does that awareness persist after the act in which it is expressed—in this case, entering the convent?

A. It is not supposed to last. But it is the simple girls who best resist the temptation to make it last. Everything in the rule of the order is in fact designed to combat the cult of the self.

Q. Does religious obedience leave, in principle, any freedom of mind whatsoever? I am thinking, in particular, of political freedom.

A. No. You do not allow yourself to judge your superiors. At election time you are very strongly advised to vote for certain political parties.

Q. It took you six months to leave the convent?

A. Six months, yes. Many novices decide to leave. After taking vows, however, very few women leave. Every resignation is treated as a special case, I think. One enters with the intention of offering blind obedience. Bear in mind that obedience is one of the three vows—along with poverty and chastity—that one prepares to take. If you doubt your vocation, you therefore continue, for a certain length of time at any rate, to trust your superior, who tells you that doubt is a common temptation.

Q. How do you overcome this contradiction?

A. The only way is to persist. I persisted for six months. I know one case where it took two years. Some people, you see, just physically cannot stand the convent life. In such cases the superior decades that you should leave. But in the kinds of cases I'm talking about, dogged persistence is the only way.

Q. What happens once you're out?

A. You feel stripped, naked. But you continue for a long time to be obsessed with both the convent life and the ideal you've renounced, even though you were absolutely determined to re-nounce it. Because if you really threw yourself into the experi-ence, you were totally invested—totally. For example, the time you spend in choir (seven or eight hours per week) is not a time of rest, even if you can't say, either, that it's a time of feverish intellectual activity. Prayer is the expression of faith, and even if you believe that faith is a product of the mind, prayer is real. You can no more deny its reality than you can deny the reality of other products of the human mind.

Q. What sort of nostalgia does the love of God leave behind, and what possible compensations are there for that love?

A. You're talking about a state of mind that has become so foreign to me that I find it difficult to talk about. When I lost the faith, I suffered because I was no longer able to pray. I no longer had anyone to whom I could address my prayers. The only equivalent I see is the absolute and definitive despair that one feels when love comes to an end.

France-Observateur, 1958

The Path of Joyful Despair

Whenever Marguerite Duras makes a film, the enthusiasm of her loyal admirers is invariably countered by the exasperation of her no less loyal detractors. *Le Monde* has always stressed the importance of Duras's cinematographic oeuvre, unlike any other because it remains ahead of, or indifferent to, all other work being done in film in France. *Le Camion* (*The Truck*, chosen to represent France at the Cannes Film Festival) and *Baxter, Vera Baxter* appeared at almost the same time. The screenplay of *Le Camion* has been published by Editions de Minuit, for Marguerite Duras's films are, in the first place, texts.

Marguerite Duras lavishes a great deal of attention on life and people. She has a philosophy all her own and speaks of the transition from writing to images in terms that change forever the way one looks at television and film and listens to the radio. In this interview she says nothing about the substantial difficulties of making films on ridiculously small budgets. She has been writing screenplays for almost twenty years (*Hiroshima mon amour* appeared in 1959) and has been a film-maker for the past eleven years. She has directed eleven films, from *La Musica* to *Le Camion*. We count on her passion, on her willingness to fight hard in order to do with almost nothing what others have been

1 3 5

incapable of doing with millions. About this interview, which might have been entitled "Film and Politics: The Same Thing," she remarks that "one must try to move from dismal despair to joyful despair."

Claire Devarrieux

Q. How does one come up with a film that relies entirely on words?

A. *Le Camion* does not rely entirely on words. There is one person who reads and another who listens. The truck on the highway is an image, is the image. It couldn't have been done on the stage. *Le Camion* is not acted, it is read, and it was not rehearsed. Had it been rehearsed, it would have been another film.

I don't know if *Le Camion* is a film that can be said to have been directed or edited; possibly it was only set in place. In the chain of representation there is an empty space: in general a text is learned, performed, represented. This text is read. That is what is uncertain in the *Camion* equation. I don't know what happened. I did it by instinct and discovered afterward that the representation had been eliminated. *Le Camion* is nothing but the representation of reading itself. And then there is the truck, a uniform element, always identical to itself, which runs across the screen like a staff of music.

I read *Le Camion* as I hear writing in the making. For one hears the words before they are projected onto the page. Before a sentence comes out the writer hears it. I remain within that inner space, as close as possible to the inner voice. In general, words are projected on a page and then apprehended by another person. That is theater. Here there is no theater. We do not descend toward the fragmentation of the text. The reading raises us up instead to the level of the text, to the place where it remains unsaid. In a personal relationship, in life, words are blurted out and nothing can be done about them, they can never be recaptured in film or on the stage. There is a kind of acting out in the text that uses up the words, that ages them. In *Le Camion* no one had heard the text before, except myself, of course, who wrote it. The risk was obviously very great. *Le Camion* is that risk.

As If Writing Were a Clandestine Act

This is a very rough text, whose parts are mostly interchangeable. That is very important. At any point I felt free to change anything I wanted. The film came together as it was being filmed. The script was written as the shooting progressed. That is the nature of *Le Camion*. The film is constantly in danger. Shots weren't set in advance. Even now the film is in danger of not existing. Even I, when I see it, tell myself that it's going to grind to a halt, break down. I've never shot a film in such a state of doubt. But the doubt wasn't sterile; it gave me and Gérard Depardieu that much more freedom. We didn't know where we were headed. The potential was unlimited both at the start and at the finish of this story that never took place, this story that ended before it began. Here, perhaps, you should ask a question about how the story stops.

Q. (Silence.)

A. The responsibility for stopping the story is the driver's. He refuses to accept it. The driver is also the spectator. Through him, frequently, the woman responds to the spectator. The disparity between them is the subject of the film—that the woman responds to the spectators was especially striking at Cannes. The cab of the truck was the movie theater. Everyone was locked up together in one place: the spectator and the film, the woman and the truck driver.

Q. Perhaps you should say a little more about representation.

A. In a theatrical or cinematographic representation, who speaks? Not the author, in my opinion, but the director and the actor. They take over the text. The written text, the book, is closed. At that moment in the process no one knows the scope of the text except the author. No one has yet translated it. The author's work is completely solitary, incapable of being conveyed by the director and the actors. They apprehend the text, they translate it. The author then either recognizes the work or is horrified by it. There have been cases in which I was horrified. I then had to go back to the book to find the text I had written. In *Le Camion* I've done away with these intermediaries.

When a text is performed, you're as far as can be from the author. Even when I direct my own texts, that's happened to me—except in *India Song*. In *India Song* the actors "proposed" the characters but did not embody them. The writing remains "offstage." Delphine Seyrig gave a fantastic performance in *India Song* because she presented herself to the audience not as someone named Anne-Marie Stretter but as her distant and dubitable double, as if disembodied, and she never conceived of the role as a void to be filled by acting but as if the reference to the Anne-Marie Stretter written into the text remained intact. In my other films, at night after shooting I sometimes felt that I had lost my text. I was desperate. The infinite potential of the text had been destroyed; the text had been wrested from its written state and embodied in a definitive version. To be frank, I always suffered from this transformation, this destruction of the text, and that is why I made *Le Camion*. The problem was not with the actors. I had the best. I had Claudine Gabey for Vera Baxter. No, it is as if writing were a clandestine act, and once speech took over that clandestinity was gone.

Q. What about *Le Camion*, then?

A. An actor sits down with the text, takes it in hand. He is never behind the text. When I read I am at one with my text. In *Le Camion* the reading is not in any sense directed. It is simply reading. And what I am trying to render is what I hear when I write, what I've always called the inner voice. If people refuse to accept *Le Camion*, they are refusing to accept both the nature of the text and the way in which it is read. Their rejection is therefore total.

I never go to the movies anymore because of the way the text and its narration are taken over by the actors and the director. I don't say this lightly. There is a thousand-year tradition of the theater behind us. Millennia of power behind us.

Q. Is it the same power?

A. It's power, yes. There is no difference between what you see every night on television and commercial films. No difference between politicians, in power or out, and the kind of acting that actors are forced to do. Occasionally the play-acting stops, but very rarely. It happened, for instance, when [former Prime Minister Pierre] Mendès France spoke the other day. A truly astonishing thing: someone who wasn't telling lies. The others are representatives, that is, actors. Actors and politicians are delegates; they are no longer themselves. They are selling their wares. The good actor is the one who sells the best, who becomes the exclusive spokesman for his line of goods. A few are not mountebanks. They are involved, like Mendès France, in a sort of distraction of representation.

Film and politics are the same thing. It's all show business. Film is show business and politics is show business—whether it's entertaining or not. For many people it is just entertainment. There is the same initial hiatus—I was going to say the same lie—in both political representation and commercial filmmaking.

Speaking in the name of an established power is no different from speaking in the name of a power yet to come. The possibility of error is completely banished from political discourse. They all know the ideal solution, they're all saviors, they're all wholly in possession of what I call the political answer. They all claim to have a radical solution to our problems and hence to deserve power. The same claim is made by classical actors. It is the claim that underlies the rhetoric of the theater and the purely psychological method of film actors, the claim that they, the representatives, possess the truth about the role, the truth about the future. No greater claim can be made.

Perhaps we ought to abandon this fixed, rationalistic, European belief in the need for a political solution. Perhaps we ought to give up on the idea that the individual should be taken in charge by the state, whatever its nature: that is a trap. The fear, the terror, that people have of being abandoned to themselves is a learned fear. People see the answer in a political program or party. They would rather have a program of any kind than no program at all; they prefer political leadership, trickery, and deceit to no solution at all. But the solution offered by the politicians in power is absolutely the same as the solution offered by the politicians in opposition.

Cinema and theater are everywhere, in the opposition as well as the majority. Perhaps we've come to the end of an era. The political lie is obvious everywhere. Why shouldn't the journalistic and cinematographic lies be denounced in the same way?

Q. The woman in *Le Camion* says: "Let the world go to its destruction—that's the only policy." What does that mean?

A. There is an ambiguity. "Let the world go to its destruction—that's the only policy" is not a profession of anarchist faith. It's an option. A destruction of the political idea, of political demands. I prefer a void, a real void, to the mess, the gigantic garbage heap, of twentieth-century ideology. I prefer no state at all, an absence of power, to the fraudulent, false, mendacious claim that a democratic state, a socialist form of government, is possible, when all the experience of the past fifty years contradicts that possibility.

The political despair that I feel, that we all feel, is becoming a cliché of the cinema. Films are awash with political despair, from Italian neo-realism to American necro-realism. I am calm, everyone else is desperate—it's becoming a common condition. An addiction to the past of the most dangerous sort. We've got to get beyond this, in my opinion. We've been taught since childhood that we should strive to give meaning to life—to the life we lead and the life we are offered. We must get over this. And we must be gay about it.

Q. How can we be gay about it?

A. The key is this: we are taught to be afraid of emptiness, of disorder. We must get over this. When a person has overcome this fear, he or she saps all the powers that be. All things are equivalent; the only way out for the individual is to recognize the fundamental sameness of the political solutions and the commercial art that are on offer. The fear must be diminished. Wherever fear exists, power has a hold. There is a direct relationship between fear and power.

The Spectator Is the Issue

The truck driver in *Le Camion* has subscribed once and for all to a solution proposed by the French Communist party. He stifles every spark of intellectual freedom he has. How does one come to such a state, to such willingness to accept the tutelage of political parties and trade unions? That is the problem of the proletariat, and it is the problem raised in the film. The truck driver is summed up in his definition, he is wholly alienated. How did the working class get itself into such a position? Into a position where it refused to participate in the spirit of May '68? Into a position where it refused life itself, refused to live? To be a member of the French Communist party is to be apolitical.

I don't know what the political future holds for France, and I don't know what the future of French film will be. I don't care. If I had the slightest idea about the future, I would still be behaving as though I possessed power; my judgment would still be swayed by power. *Le Camion* is an act not of power but of the cinema.

Q. And the woman in *Le Camion?*

A. This woman—faceless, identityless, classless, possibly an escapee from a lunatic asylum, who imagines that she is the mother of all the Jewish children killed at Auschwitz or that she is a Portuguese or an Arab or a Malian, this woman who reinvents everything that she has ever learned—this woman is for me a woman who is open to the future. If she is mad, so much the better: may everyone be as mad as she is. I use the word *mad* as the spectator understands it. The spectator needs to recognize before he can judge. If he does not recognize this woman, if he does not recognize her attraction to all forms of oppression—an attraction I call love—then I can do nothing for him, nothing to help him join her. The spectator is the issue, just as the political activist is the issue. Both are responsible.

If, like the truck driver, the spectator "eyeballs" the woman and demands that she have a recognizable and reassuring identity, then to my mind both driver and spectator are swallowed up in the same darkness, the same terrifying political night.

Le Camion makes an issue of the responsibility of the working class as well as of the spectator, the class of spectators. The working class, too, has been stuck, broken down, for decades. The spectator is responsible for subjecting himself to all the powers, to all the ideologies. He is defined by his dependency, by his fantastic equation of endurance.

Vera Baxter, Woman of the Medieval Forests

Q. Who is Vera Baxter in the film?

A. I repeat what I have said before: that Vera Baxter is a devilish woman, devoured by her fidelity. Possibly a hopeless case. I know, we all know, that such cases exist. She is devilish because of her one-sided devotion to marriage and fidelity. Or perhaps I'm mistaken. Perhaps desire is desire for one person. Perhaps desire is the opposite of the scattering of desire.

What I know about Vera Baxter is that her life, on the surface, is completely reassuring and normal. She is, in every country of the world, the very image of the perfect wife and mother, and she frightens me. I'm not frightened of the woman in *Le Camion*. The woman in *Le Camion* is not hemmed in by any identity. She has shed all possible identities, she has ceased to be anything other than a hitchhiker. There are those who claim to be in possession of what they call "theoretical praxis," Marxist or some other. This woman is in possession of the praxis of hitchhiking.

Vera Baxter, before the film starts, is apparently helpless. She is disabled by love, if you will. But in the film Vera Baxter is the victim of an accident—the accident of desire. Jean Baxter pays a stranger so that his wife will stop being faithful to him; that comes under the heading of desire. Vera Baxter's adultery, bought and paid for, is supposed to reap a rich return, by reviving the couple's desire. But the expected result does not come about. Vera Baxter, launched into prostitution (whether paid or not), will never go back to Jean Baxter. Possibly she'll die as a result. I mean she will die of not loving one man until death do them part. I believe that she wants to kill herself, simply because it is possible not to love one man for one's entire life. Therein lies the profoundly archaic side of Vera Baxter's character. She is a woman of the medieval forests: there are millions of them loose in our world.

I think that if Vera Baxter ever met the woman from *Le Camion*, she would be afraid, but she wouldn't define the woman, as the truck driver does, in stereotyped political terms. What the two women share in common, probably irremediably, is love. We have long been told of Vera Baxter's love for her children and her husband. We know less about the amorphous, anarchic, dangerous love of the woman from *Le Camion*. To love one child and to love all children, whether living or dead— somewhere these two loves come together. To love a no-good but humble punk and to love an honest man who believes himself to be an honest man—somewhere these, too, come together.

Le Monde, 1977

This Large, Black Animal

This essay is written in homage to *Koko, the Talking Ape*, a marvelous film made by Barbet Shroeder in 1978.

This large animal, still young, black in color, is of an ugliness so beautiful, so great, that we are forced to admit that perhaps beauty has ceased to be the essential ingredient of film that it has been for the past fifty years. Why is it that when this black animal is on screen, she is more present than any human being, even the most famous of international film stars? Koko is what they call her, the way some people use the words *nigger* or *a-rab*. I shall call her Africa. Why does Africa occupy the screen in such an incomparable way that not even the most penetrating analysis can possibly convey the sovereignty of her image? of her presence? of her difference from us, whom she so closely resembles? "Ugly as an ape," they say. Africa, in my opinion, is the ugliest of animals, uglier than the elephant or the camel, uglier than any woman declared ugly by human society. So what is it that happens when

Africa is on screen that does not happen when other species—
species of obvious, human splendor such as tigers and panthers—
appear on the same screen?

We all know what happens, I think: Africa is a gorilla, an anthropoid, the largest of all the anthropoids but closest to us,
standing on the other shore. She is as far from us as from her fore-
bears. And we—we are as far from her as from the void that
stands before us. If an image is wanted, perhaps a river will do.
On one bank stands anthropos, alone. On the other, Africa the
anthropoid, equally alone. We look at each other. Between us
stand a billion years. Africa's solitude in the chain of being is also
our solitude. Africa's solitude. Some say she should be left there,
that Africa's solitude ought to be respected. But if Africa were left
to her solitude, she would already have ceased to exist. Gorilla
meat is prized by the people of Gabon, and mummified gorilla
heads fetch high prices from European tourists.

That's the way it is. There are no more than six thousand gorillas left in the world. Millions have been slaughtered. Ten years
ago there were five hundred tigers in Bengal, now there are
no more than forty. It's all over. Any statement of the problem,
any information about the problem, is suspect in advance. Why
should you be right? Why should we be wrong? No one knows
what has to be done to save us, to save the gorillas, the whales,
the ocean, childhood, swallows, love. No one. So why then—it's
not my reaction—why decree that Africa must remain for ever
and ever nothing but a subject for documentary, grist for *The
Wide World of Animals*, much as the Negro dances of Central Africa have for decades been grist for presidential visits—European
presidential visits? Shouldn't we teach Africa to be suspicious of
men? Shouldn't we, therefore, bring her to us?

When Africa is on screen—Africa, a gigantic child hamstrung
by her own strength, a prehistoric Garbo unaware that she is a
Garbo—the truth is apparent: Africa bears within her an immensity—the species, in its innocence as well as its tragedy. Africa
doesn't see well. She can't tell things apart. When asked in the
morning "How are you?" she sometimes answers, "Sad." "Why
sad?" they ask, and she answers that she doesn't know why she is
sad. Africa draws the word *sad* on her face in the sign language of

the deaf, two fingers along the tracks of her tears, two straight lines that fall from her eyes toward the center of the earth. A miracle: Africa does not know how to be sad with a sadness that she shares with us. She does not know how to be sad with sadness, melancholy with melancholy, beyond all knowledge.

Le Matin de Paris, 1978

Knowledge of Horror: *L'Etabli,*
by Robert Linhart

When you've finished reading this book, you feel like proclaiming it the one true political act that has been accomplished in France in years. You want to share it, read it to others, to everyone, to children, students, women. To workers. This is what one might call a reader's book, by someone who is not writing *about* the condition of workers but is writing it *down,* a book by a person who is not making a career of writing, who is not an author. A book that looks like no one made it, possibly the first and the last "communist" book—the word suddenly stands out, in stark isolation.

The writer of *L'Etabli* [*The Workbench*] is a professor of philosophy. In 1969 he spent a year working on the assembly line in the Citroën plant at Porte de Choisy. Eight years later he wrote *L'Etabli.* The book is about a year in the life of the factory, as seen by Robert Linhart in the course of his involuntary journey from shop to shop in the Citroën division that makes the charming, universally loved 2CV. Linhart's lack of manual dexterity—

his manual stupidity, one might say—constituted a tragic flaw in a world dominated by the manual genius of those fated to do this kind of work: the damned of the earth, the workers of the Third World. On the assembly line he could not keep up. He was shuffled from one shop to another (a semiskilled worker, paid four francs an hour, is never sacked—they can always find something for him to do): from the welding shop ("unable to keep up") to the door shop ("unable to keep up") to the seat shop ("works too slowly") to the very quiet Panhard warehouse, Citroën's morgue, and finally to an assignment delivering 2CV chassis to a staging area in the factory, where he made the acquaintance of Ali, a lonely Moroccan worker, "an obstinate and solitary striker" who, because he refused to *give* his employer three-quarters of an hour of extra work per day in compensation for advances made to the workers in May '68, found himself assigned to the job of cleaning toilets in the plant at Javel. It is to Ali, the son of a Muslim saint and Arabic poet, who, as an anti-Semite, embodies the painful contradiction between political intelligence and the intelligence of freedom, that Robert Linhart's book is dedicated.

The book follows the course of a job action at Citroën: the creation of a grass-roots committee to represent workers at the Choisy plant. Every day there was a strike: workers refused to work the extra three-quarters of an hour required by the company. The strike enjoyed fairly widespread support (at first by organized groups, later by scattered individuals) despite the terrifying risks involved. The strikers had to fight the C.F.T., Citroën's yellow-dog union, with its thugs and informers. The strike was lost in advance, but the workers went ahead with it just the same. It was a strike in opposition to any organization that claimed to monopolize the right to analyze the political situation. In other words, it was a strike undertaken on unreasonable, utopian grounds, just like May '68—and for that reason I imagine that many errant leftists, and perhaps even the author of *L'Etabli*, will recognize themselves in it. This strike was the result of unfortunate political ignorance (in my day we called it "deviation"). The workers should have waited for orders from the specialists. But here instinct born of anger was so powerful, so imperious, that nothing could tame it. The workers were deaf and blind. Anger—whether of workers or women or men or intellectuals or readers or animals or thinkers—is the anger of knowledge, of the inability of knowledge to express itself. Moses was so possessed by the idea of God that he could do nothing but shout. He had lost his powers of speech, of compromise, of common sense. No choice: it's either this, or kill, or die.

You may think you know what a factory is. You don't know anything of the kind. You may think you know what it is to be a woman or a child or a black or a Malian working at Citroën. But you don't know. You're caught, buried, in such coils of rhetoric that you've ceased even to understand yourself. What concern people show for us! Everybody would like to *teach* us to "imagine" political events, to judge politics according to standard norms. Then, suddenly, a book like *L'Etabli* appears—at last, a personal response. *L'Etabli* marks a step forward for everything that is unknown in the world, and hence for all causes at once. At the same time it strikes a telling blow at what is called "interpretation of the facts"—an epidemic, increasingly difficult to tolerate. Interpretation—whether of a miscellaneous crime or a miscellaneous political fact. The one final, ultimate form of stupidity is the certainty that one is in possession of true knowledge. To know that one does not know: *L'Etabli* reestablishes the pristine original meaning of the phrase.

When one thinks of the Citroën plant at Choisy in 1969 or of the plant at Javel today or of other plants in Berlin or Turin or wherever—prisons in which immigrants by the thousands are incarcerated—it is laughable that so much attention is paid to whether or not those plants are nationalized. Who cares? It is laughable, too, that Marxist theory is so focused on the critique of local and international working conditions and that Marxist theoreticians believe that without them we could never understand the plain truth: that nine-tenths of the world's people are at the mercy of the wealthy one-tenth.

Labor today means an unstanchable flow, a hemorrhage, of hungry workers ready to put up with anything in order to earn enough to eat. The factories open the flood gates and workers flow in; they close the flood gates and the flow of workers halts. Native proletariats quit the factories and are replaced by an infinitely malleable work force, whose only morality is compounded of hunger and fear.

This is the essence of the political picture today, this nameless *thing*, this human materiel—the worker who, in order to survive, is obliged to *give* half his time to international capitalism. Because "surplus value" has been given a name, we think we understand it, but we never do—we understand less and less as time goes by.

The factory is creating new misfortunes for the working class. Man's atrocity as well as his martyrdom stands revealed. The managers of the assembly line at Citroën-Choisy—supervisors, foremen, and timekeepers, men owned lock, stock, and barrel by the company—are as doomed as the upper echelons of the police, subject to replacement by the workers themselves. In the Paris area the French lord it over the Portuguese and the Portuguese lord it over the blacks. The chain of despair is endless. Once hunger is satisfied there comes this new misfortune, and the worker feels less well off than when he was ready.

L'Etabli reads like a horror story, a work of terror. Those who profit from this intolerable world are like the kingpins of real estate or the drug trade: we see them only on television, freshly polished and shaved. But what's happening? Lately, amidst the trash of the recent political campaigns, the young wolves of the world have seemed more afraid of losing their power than the beggars of losing their bread. What horror in such misery!

L'Etabli. I greet its publication as I would greet the coming of spring. For us it is springtime. For knowledge of the horror is, in its own way, refreshing. The wonderful concreteness of desperation sweeps away all theory. Leave me alone, says the child, I'm reading. When the book has been put aside, one wants to be alone. Its incomparable power can be summed up thus: when you've finished reading you no longer know what to think. This book does not go away. It stays with you like an idle thought, a thought not yet fully framed, yet sure to determine all the others.

Libération, 1978

The Rags of Salonika: Z, by Vassilis Vassilikos

"When a people is not allowed to speak," says Vassilis Vassilikos, "everything that it does is lost. You have a hundred films about your resistance against the Nazis. We have two about ours. And you didn't have a civil war . . ."

That is why he wrote Z.

Z stands for *zei:* He lives. Who? Lambrakis, a left-wing politician assassinated on 22 May 1965 in Salonika. A dense and admirable work, Z fully achieves its purpose: to shed light on a moment of considerable importance in history—which to be sure did not pass unnoticed, but which, had nothing been done, would have ended buried in a shroud of time. Is Z a novel? No. A document? No. It is a grandiose, exhaustive, modern account of political reality. One is profoundly glad that this book was written and, now that it has been smuggled out of the concentration camp that is contemporary Greece, cannot be destroyed.*

*In 1967, when these words were written, Greece was ruled by a military junta.—Trans.

"The event is one that for us has not yet ended," says Vassilikos. "The proof is that Mr. Kolias, prosecutor in the case, is now prime minister of Greece, while Mikis Theodorakis, president of the Lambrakis Youth, an organization of some 200,000 young Greeks, is today in prison. In discussing this assassination I lacked what is called historical perspective. Lambrakis was our Che, our Lumumba, our Malcolm X, our Ben Barka.

"This was an event that shaped us, that determined our future and even our political consciousness. We were brutalized by the dreadful propaganda of the extreme right, born of collaboration with the Nazis and of the civil war. To be sure, there were other, similar assassinations. But the Lambrakis case was the most clear-cut. It laid bare the structure of the new Greek society, the 'perennial' rule of the right, the total contempt for the aspirations of the Greek people, the sharing of power by a handful of cliques that changed their political stripes whenever it was expedient, the perpetuation of semicolonial conditions (the only difference between Greece and Latin America is that in Greece there are no latifundia), and the use of the lumpen proletariat by the police."

Chance Passersby

Lambrakis's killers came from this lumpen proletariat (as did his champions). They came from the Ano Tumba district of Salonika, which since 1922 has been inhabited by unemployed illiterates. The assassins had lived together for twenty-two years in chaos, ignorance, and poverty. Heroes were killed. Anyone who dared to speak up went to prison. The owning and ruling class knew nothing of the seething life beneath it. Whenever there was a disturbance the government stepped in to put it down. The corruption of the police was taken for granted. Nothing, not even selling from a pushcart, could be done without payment of bribes. The people lived in silence. Fear was the one common denominator. And then, one day, Lambrakis appeared. A miracle: he belonged to the class that possessed the power of speech, and he betrayed it.

How can one explain his assassination? How can one describe the slaying of nascent hope? Can one blame the affection, the love, that the Greek people felt for its deputy? For twenty years he breathed his speeches. Vassilikos begins by describing the murder from the point of view of the two assassins and of Z himself. First Lambrakis was bludgeoned as he entered the Club of the Friends of Peace. Then, outside the club, he was run over by a delivery wagon. A hysterical crowd ringed the premises. In it were members of the Organization (an association of victims of the Greek resistance against the Germans). The men behind the crime, the killers, the imbeciles, the chief of the Athens police were all there—all "who shout but have nothing to say."

But there were also the chance passersby, and Hatsis. Nobody and everybody—unpredictable, indefatigable: a cabinet maker, a tailor, a driver, a student. And Hatsis: an admirable, unforgettable character, "by turns a mason, painter, water carrier, and shoeshine boy, a bald man, a malingerer, who loved Z in much the same way as a soccer fan loves a soccer player . . . for his lonely march the month before to Marathon and for his having punched a socialist deputy in the eye." He had walked all day to be there, next to Z. He was there.

Witnesses

Vassilikos does not use the testimony of the Friends of Peace. He uses that of the passersby, and of Hatsis. And as each witness testifies, he describes once more the death of Z. Some didn't understand at first what was happening. Others understood something right away. Still others grasped it all within a few seconds. As each witness speaks, Lambrakis dies yet again. His death is cumulative, each time more profound, more terrifying. Death seen by ignorance, by cowardice, and by the intelligence of Hatsis, who like a bolt of lightning rends nineteen centuries of darkness, for one brief moment defying the political intelligence of the professional politicians.

The vast plot mounted by the police and the Organization—an "accident"—was thus attacked from all sides by secondary accidents, all of which converged toward a point that at first seemed quite remote but gradually drew nearer and nearer: the truth. It is as though Lambrakis's death *acted*, transformed itself into an active force. It acts on us in the same way. We cannot put the book down. We become witnesses of Z's death.

In recounting the trial, Vassilikos again uses the device of presenting the testimony of many witnesses. Once more we encounter the witnesses who were at the club. Again there is terror on every page: not terror that they will be killed before they testify, but terror that they will *waver*. They come from Salonika in rags. They have nothing to say but the truth. They are afraid for their families. Ants—but there are a lot of them, already there are quite a few. They seek out judges and journalists in order to speak.

Another story admirably told. We are afraid that no one will listen, that no one will have the patience to hear them out. Money is frightening. It is offered to them. Millions of drachmas are offered to Hatsis and Nikitas, the cabinet maker, and the time that it takes to find out whether or not they will accept those millions, enough to live the rest of their lives in comfort beyond their wildest dreams, is more unbearable than if they were flayed alive.

The same fear grips you as you read about the judges and journalists. One judge, "a judge like any other judge," we are told, but honest, disciplined in the law, is a hero. One outraged journalist, who ignores orders, threats, and bribes, is a hero. We are witnessing the beginning of a civilization. On one side, the people, standing together. On the other, the rulers and the owners, a conspiracy. Between the two camps stands the judge, the only man possessed of a modern sense of conscience. "Surrounded by those above him and by the masses who turned their eyes toward him as toward their only savior . . . the judge, drunk with stubbornness and fatigue, steadfastly made his way across the rotten ground where everything is mixed up with everything else."

The journalist, Antoniou, "is certain of one thing: that the entire city is involved in the crime." He, too, pursues the evidence and finds things out. Antoniou—alone, perhaps, of eight hundred journalists?—was struck by the cabinet maker's testimony, and he helps us pursue the truth to the bitter end.

I was bothered at first by the lyricism with which Vassilikos describes the pain of Greece, of Z, of Z's widow, and also of his "soul," but in the end I was won over, because that lyricism seemed to me the only possible counterpoint to the realism of the witnesses' testimony. And such realism was the only way to wrest the truth, strand by strand, from the morass. Vassilikos is not a naïf. And when he is, it is because he wants or wanted to be. This is an epic tale, a tale of courage, of heroism, of the quest for truth. Through Z the 400,000 Greeks who awaited the body of Lambrakis at the Athens railway station speak, along with the witnesses, the killers, the traitors, and the heroes. It was inevitable that the book Z, which through these many voices proclaims the curse of being Greek in the year nineteen hundred and sixty-seven, would be banned in Greece. It has been since last April.

Le Nouvel Observateur, 1967

Othon, by Jean-Marie Straub

Let's take the risk of plunging into film without asking permission. Let's invent our own standards and trust only in spontaneous criticism, which does exist. There are quite a few of us who believe in nothing else. Quite a few of us who see the names Carl Theodor Dreyer or Jean-Marie Straub on a poster or in a flier and go to see their films. They are filmmakers whose films the professional critics forbid us to see. That alone is reason enough to go see them.

In 1964 one of the great film masterpieces, Dreyer's *Gertrud,* was killed and buried by the critics (it played in Paris for one week). Who was responsible? You, who believed the critics. Too late.

Attention! *Othon,** the fifth and last film of Jean-Marie Straub,† opened on 13 January in Paris. You have two weeks to

*The full title of the film, which is directly inspired by Pierre Corneille's play, is *Les yeux ne veulent pas en tout temps se fermer,* or *Peut-être qu'un jour Rome se permettra de choisir à son tour.*

†Jean-Marie Straub is French. His films (including *Chronique d'Anna Mag-*

see it. When that time is up, if the box office receipts aren't high enough, *Othon* will close. Attention! It is difficult to believe that the professional critics are capable of judging *Othon*. Very likely they can neither see nor hear nor perceive in any way the nature of Straub's project and work. This is a kind of film they will not recognize. A text of pure intelligence that they will not recognize. The choice is theirs, and from their judgment there is no appeal. But they shun the freedom they've been given.

I am speaking to you, people I don't know. I do not know how you will respond to Straub's film. My only reason for speaking to you about *Othon* is to do what I can to make sure it won't suffer the same fate as *Gertrud*.

What I, Marguerite Duras, see is this: *Othon* has been exhumed from the tomb in which it has lain since 1708; Straub has traveled back in time to restore it to its nascent state. Miraculously I see the man from Rouen [Pierre Corneille] in a rage against the authorities as he writes his play. I understand why it was no accident that, between 1682 and 1708, the Comédie Française performed the play only thirty times; I understand that it is a play about power and its internal contradictions. I did not know this. I used to think that Corneille, Shakespeare, and Racine (excepting [director Roger] Planchon's [version of Racine's] *Bérénice*) slept covered with dust, drowned out by the sempiternal maundering of "culture," so that their voices could no longer be heard, their dramas no longer seen. When I saw *Othon*, the violence of the play was such that I forgot Corneille and Straub. That's the first time such a thing has happened to me.

To call a work obscure is just as disastrous as to call it a masterpiece of clarity: the text becomes burdened with a prejudice that prevents the reader from relating to it directly. The work is imprisoned. Straub has opened the doors of both prisons. *Othon* appears liberated from all visions prior to your own. Corneille's spectators are not accustomed to such freedom. Some will mistake it for a difficulty of Straub's work. Here the text is not recited to please the spectator. It is spoken neither well nor badly: it is

dalena Bach, released in Paris), are German. Because Straub refused to fight in Algeria, he was forced into exile. The army still dogs his footsteps. He is thirty-eight years old. Such is the situation of the man whom many of us regard as today's leading filmmaker.

the inner voice that speaks. Here the versification does not serve to puff up or intoxicate the actors; they do not use the words as mouthwash.

The text is a dialectical development, a respiratory rhythm, a white space. This suggests that theater is everywhere where there is speech. And that beneath the surface of the political texts that seem least poetic—Saint-Just or Marx, for example—there lies the beat of the Cornelian contrabass. All accents are allowed except that of the Comédie Française—in other words, the accent of camouflaged meaning, of authority. The framing here is done by words. The ceremonial inherited from tragedy, the emphatic gestures have been eliminated: here there is nothing useless, everything is to the point. The universality of the meaning is recaptured. Straub has traveled through time to rediscover Corneille. He has broken the link between tragedy and its literal historical meaning, established once and for all by rationalist culture.

In other words, he has restored tragedy's subversive dimension. His work is an extraordinary work of healing, of resurrection. For three centuries *Othon* has been the victim of a crime. Here is *Othon* restored to youth. Subversion there is, outside as well as inside. Now that the film is finished, one can see this. On the Palatine hill in Rome in the year 69. This high ground plays a part in space and time. The scenic space is circumscribed by the automobile traffic of contemporary Rome: an imperturbable flow that gradually comes to seem a pure movement, like a river or lava flow. We hear this heavy traffic. Is there any place where one could read the text and not hear it? It would be a mistake not to hear the traffic in parallel with the text. Timeless, sacred space no longer exists. Corneille must be read now or not at all.

The power denounced here exists, just like the automobiles. As Lacus says, as men of government always say: "Let's make ourselves secure and laugh at the rest. There's no public good if things go against us. Let's live only for ourselves and think only of ourselves."

Beneath the leaden mantle of power, one free man has read Corneille: Straub.

Chronique, RTL, 1967

Seyrig-Hiss

They speak. They form the words inside their mouths, make them—within—and then, effortlessly, let them come out. Once out, the word is at first as if dumbstruck, devoid of meaning, *alone*. Then, suddenly, it takes on life, it quivers with life.

Let me try again: They speak. The words are at first contained in their mouths but with no breath of their own, no separate existence. Then they allow the words to slip smoothly out: The transition is easy, painless. The word sleeps again once it is out. Asleep, it finds itself in the open air. Then and only then does it awaken: the suffering is audible. The word unfolds, breathes, and cries. Its eventual meaning is still to come. But first this initial word must scream with surprise: what comes out is noise, a cry. What one hears first is the suffering of contact with the outside world. Taken by surprise, the infant-word refuses to be separated from them. Caught red-handed in a painfully sobering moment, it offers itself to us. Then and only then does meaning come and cloak the word, dress it up, install it in the sentence in which it will embed itself, fix itself, and die.

Let me try again: They speak. They say: "I love you so much that I'm blind. I'm deaf. I'm dying." Or: "I would like to be in your shoes, arriving here for the first time in the rain." I listen. A hundred times. The silent voices that they have (I think) only with me, of which they know nothing: an as yet untapped resource, intact, *integral, mortal.* Projecting these voices are two women who—to my great delight—suck the blood out of any privileged, *private,* circumscribed meaning. In "I love you," in "I would like to be arriving here," the word *here* drifts, it wanders about like a floating continent that might moor itself anywhere: it becomes general.

Sorcières, 1976

Delphine Seyrig, a Celebrated Unknown

Delphine Seyrig was born in Lebanon in 1932. "In the most beautiful light in the world," she says. Her father, Henri Seyrig, was the most famous French archeologist working in the Middle East. Her mother, a Genevan by birth, was a fervent admirer of Jean-Jacques Rousseau. She grew up in a Protestant environment, passionately involved with culture.

The Seyrig family left for New York when Delphine was ten. She remained there until she was fourteen. During those four—decisively influential—years, Delphine Seyrig became "American."

"I don't feel particularly French," she says. "I'm just as much American."

After spending several years in a boarding school in the Cévennes, she returned to New York and married an American: John Youngerman. They had a son, Duncan, now eleven.

At age twenty, after a peculiar course of study the need for which she says she never understood, Delphine Seyrig made her debut in the theater. She played in provincial drama centers, at

Saint-Etienne and Strasbourg (such centers, increasingly numerous, have decentralized and diversified French theatrical life over the past twenty years). Then she came to Paris to appear in a play by Louis Ducreux: *L'Amour en papier.* For eight years she appeared on stage in Paris and New York. By all appearances her career was progressing normally, which is to say, gradually. Then, suddenly, in 1961, an explosion: Alain Resnais, who often selects his actors from the legitimate theater (where he discovered Emmanuelle Riva, heroine of *Hiroshima mon amour*), noticed Delphine Seyrig. A year later this discovery resulted in *Last Year at Marienbad,* an international success.

This success had a curious result: the theater reclaimed Delphine Seyrig (except for her appearance in *Muriel,* a fine Resnais film that too few people have seen). Now, though, her name alone was enough to fill theaters. Under the direction of the amazing Claude Régy, she would go on filling theaters for the next five years.

Then, abruptly, she began doing both plays and films: Pinter and Pirandello on the one hand, François Truffaut, Joseph Losey, Klein, and myself on the other.

Today Seyrig is quite simply the greatest actress in France. "Possibly in the world," a very well-known French director said to me the other day.

Yes, I think so, too: possibly in the world.

Having given you the sterile outline of her "biography," how can I "show" her to you?

From the Protestant childhood, the cultured milieu, and the pink skies of Mount Lebanon and Baalbek came her understanding of art and of life, her austere grace, her fierce loyalty, her almost traumatic distaste for lying, and so on. The rest is from her alone.

But who is "she"?

It has been estimated that it would take hundreds of pages to describe in a rigorous manner a man's footstep, detailing the actions not only of his muscles and nerves but also of his will. How many pages would it take to describe a smile, a glance, an inflection? A thousand?

All I can do is make you want to imagine, in your own way, the woman named Delphine Seyrig.

To begin with, she never gives interviews. When I phoned her to say I wanted to write about her in *Vogue,* she panicked.

"What can you say about an actress? There is nothing to say, only something to see!"

"I can try. Are you willing?"

She agreed. In the first place, we're friends. And then, I'm not a journalist. She is terrified of journalists because "they distort the truth." She is the only actress in Europe who refuses to appear in the major magazines, because to do so one has to deal with them—the journalists.

You never see her at fashionable cocktail parties. There's never been the slightest gossip about her. She can't stand the distortion of reality by journalism—the most widely accepted and commonplace distortion there is—and she can't stand the society rituals on which journalism feeds.

So, then: You can neglect your publicity and still become a great actress.

She is tall for a Frenchwoman. She is thin. She has a very beautiful body. Very, very blue eyes. A radiant complexion. Blonde hair, usually. Brilliant teeth, slightly irregular, which she bares fully when she laughs (she was once told that she could never do films because one tooth slightly overlaps another and that she ought to have it fixed. She refused: "Never," she said. And now she says: "You see, you mustn't listen to *them*").

When she walks, her whole body moves, and she makes no more noise than a child. In France when people ask, Who walks the best? the answer is: Delphine Seyrig.

She has fast friends, staunch friendships. She is perfectly bilingual. She has a house in Paris, a real house in a superb courtyard on one of the most beautiful squares in the world, the place des Vosges, formerly the place Royale. A huge house just for her and her son, Duncan. A terrace with rosebushes. She drives like a cab driver. She has a wild laugh. She dances the jerk. She is always even-tempered in the presence of others. When she has a couple of days off, she goes to the ocean, to the Channel coast, and when she has only an afternoon off she goes to the *cinémathèque* in the place du Trocadéro [a famous library of old films, several of which are shown each day—Trans.]. She is in the streets in the afternoon, wearing a raincoat, no makeup, book in hand, in case movies should ever disappear from the face of the earth, leaving nothing to do but read until doomsday arrived. What else? No one else seems so fragile. In fact, though, she is as rugged as a North Sea sailor. She has a passionate and invisible private life. She is separated from her husband, but he is her best friend.

If you haven't seen her films, how can I tell you what she has done for the cinema?

Listen: when Delphine Seyrig comes into camera range, the shades of Garbo and Clara Bow pass the lens and you look for Cary Grant at her side. You feel sad at the chaotic state of film today. Her thin face is as unpredictable as that of a woman passing in the street; it owes nothing to any fashion, and upon it lies the smile of an all-embracing good humor or intelligence. The face remains unpredictable no matter how often one sees it. She calls it "variety."

"I don't believe in 'jobs.' You change when you want to change. You have to take one thing at a time, one film at a time, one play at a time. But you have to perform. Above all, perform. Don't think about your career but about the thing you're doing or are about to do. The thing is not to line up 'jobs' but to remain entirely open to the part."

That brings us to what ultimately separates her from other actresses: her way of speaking.

"People say I have a funny way of speaking, and it's true, I talk funny, but that's the way I talk in real life."

It's true. There's no difference between the voice of the actress and that of the mother as she speaks to the little boy who shares her house.

I've hit upon an image, and I'll share it with you: she speaks like someone who has just learned French, who has a fantastic aptitude for French but no experience speaking the language, and who feels an extreme, physical pleasure in speaking it. She sounds as though she has just eaten a piece of fruit and her mouth is still moist with it. The words and the sentences and the speeches form in the resulting freshness, bittersweet, green, springlike, and when they reach our ears they are uniquely rejuvenated.

They tell me that she speaks English the same way—inimitably.

I personally would hire her from her telephone voice alone, sight unseen.

Some people can't stand her voice, though their numbers are diminishing. Others are intoxicated by it. As for me, before I let other people read any text of mine, I "hear" it read by Delphine.

This unrealistic voice, with its absolutely unpredictable punctuation, counter to every rule—this, too, is Delphine Seyrig.

Are you beginning to invent an image of her?

Imagine some impossible genealogies. Whose granddaughter might Jeanne Moreau be? I would say Stendhal's, via Louis Malle. And Delphine? Proust's, via Alain Resnais. Continue the game. When and where might Jeanne Moreau have been born? I would say in the country, in France, in Burgundy, during the Restoration. And Delphine? In romantic Arabia, on the edge of the desert where T. E. Lawrence roamed. The one is French, the other—you can't say exactly where she comes from.

She has one foot in New York throughout the year. And I mean New York: the city, with its theaters, streets, dirt, strikes, blacks, madmen, and movie theaters.

"If I had nothing else to do, nothing at all, I'd like to sell tickets at a movie theater. That way I could see the films."

I respond that I would like to manage a filling station along a major highway with lots of traffic.

"That's not bad either. Listen (pause). I'd like once in my life to do Shakespeare in English."

Are you beginning to invent a voice? To see a face?

Listen again: once I worked with her for a month on a film. I saw her every day, in happiness and in sadness, when she got up in the morning and when she went to bed at night, in exasperation, fatigue, anxiety, what have you. I never saw her inflict her mood on others. Never.

I'll say more: Whatever happened to other people, whether good or ill, she shared as I have never seen anyone share joys and sorrows.

Once, in the course of making this film, one of the technicians was treated unfairly. It had nothing to do with her. She shouted. And she cried.

"I know it has nothing to do with me, but I can't, I can't stop myself."

The only hindrance to her freedom is the injustice of which other people are victims.

Vogue, 1969

Jeanne Moreau

"An actor," she says, "is made to utter words. An actor is a mouth that opens to speak words written by others. An actor is made to be seen."

Therein lies a crucial difference between writers and actors. Writers know nothing of the actor's total physical involvement. You use your body, your face, everything that is given to you *at birth* in order to be an actress. An actor must please the audience. He must seduce those who look at him, above all else.

That was how the interview began.

She is not very tall. She is very, very thin. Ninety-nine pounds. No matter what the season she has golden skin—an extraordinarily fine complexion. Her mouth looks like a segment of an orange. Her eyes are bronzed. They are as soft as silk. Her gaze is one of relentless intelligence. Intelligent before she was a star, intelligent she still is. Her conversation embraces all subjects, without a trace of hypocrisy.

"When you're an actress," she says, "you're constantly in the emotional situation of a woman ready to experience the greatest love of her life. All the weapons of a woman in love—an actress uses them."

Love, she says, is an ever-present part of her life. Whether it is love to come or present love or love in the fullness of its discovery or love on the wane, love is always part of her life.

"When I'm involved in a major love affair, it of course affects my pleasure in acting," she says. "My senses are awakened, alert. But the love that I portray in my films is always exemplary compared to the love that I experience."

If she plays a part on stage while in love, does she feel that she is performing for "him"?

"Never. I never play for him alone. Thanks to him my senses are extraordinarily alive, but at the same time I elude his grasp. Thanks to him I perform better. And because I perform better, I forget him, I throw myself even more into my role, and I elude him all the more."

To which she adds: "That, you see, is the actor's infidelity."

She has small hands, beautifully modeled. Sometimes "she wears rings on every finger," between the first and second joints, a little girl's rings. Her friend Louise de Vilmorin taught her the style.

"Why should you throw out your childhood rings?" she asks. "Wear them higher up, almost at your fintertips. Like this."

What would she have done with those hands if stardom had not preserved them?

"If a war or some other unforeseeable event forced me to stop acting, I can see myself working in the fields, growing things to eat."

She has told me this repeatedly. The work she would have liked to do would have been manual work; she wouldn't have liked being idle. We talk sometimes about weddings and banquets in rural restaurants, how calm it is afterward, and how deeply one sleeps. We talk about the joy of feeding the world, and about the nostalgia we feel for a traditional family life lived according to the rules.

Admired as no other woman is admired, constantly surrounded by admirers, she brings up the question of the loneliness of women.

In the quiet rue des Missionnaires in Versailles, in a residential enclave, she lives alone, with Anna, her housekeeper, and Albert, her chauffeur. Her son, Jérôme, comes home only for vacations; the rest of the time he is away at boarding school in Switzerland.

What defines solitude? Something insignificant, perhaps. Is it the mere fact of returning alone from Paris in the back seat of her Rolls-Royce? Is it dining alone? Is it being alone late at night?

Is it the terror of sitting down at a table where only one place is set? The terror of summer travels?

We talked about it.

"Go to Greece alone? I'd rather stay in my room."

We laughed about it. Not being alone, we said, "also" meant not being alone when it came to paying the telephone bill, the rent, or the garage mechanic. It "also" meant being tied economically to a man.

Yet the illusion remained perfect. Jeanne said, "I could never stay alone."

And as she uttered these words she was living in the loneliness she denounced. Jeanne has also known the "loneliness à deux" of the couple, an often distressing loneliness to which one nevertheless becomes addicted. She had a child in her marriage. Jean Richard—who is still her best friend—was poor. They loved each other in years of difficulty, of intense work, of common passion for their profession, the theater.

But they were too young. Stardom came to Jeanne like a bolt out of the blue, as has happened to actresses the world over.

Is it possible to have so many friends and still be alone? Surely. Jeanne has friends. She calls us "her world."

"I constantly need to feel my world around me," she says. "It must be there, near or far, but it must always exist. There is only one exception: the few weeks prior to shooting a film. Then I have to leave my friends and become a stranger, another person, dedicated to an existence different from my own."

The world around Jeanne is quite solid, quite strong. That we go for weeks sometimes, or even for months, without seeing each other—during shooting, for example—never affects our loyalty to one another. When she needs us or we need her, we are there and she is there. Florence Malraux, Danièle and Serge Rezvani, the painter, François Truffaut, and others.

From time to time she invites us—in groups—to her home in

Versailles. She cooks dishes that she invents herself. She receives us as a queen receives kings, with extraordinary attention and affection. After dinner Serge Rezvani takes his guitar and sings his songs. Sometimes Jeanne's mother, Kathlin, is there, a former Blue Bell Girl from the Casino de Paris. Sometimes her younger sister, Michèle, who owns a restaurant in London. More often we find her father, Anatole Désiré Moreau, the farmer from Allier.

Then she goes off again to make another film, and each new film is a great strain on her nerves. When it's over, as she says herself, she feels like a convalescent in both a physical and a spiritual sense.

Her films tear her apart. Her films are perhaps the primary cause of that solitude of which I spoke earlier. A terrible contradiction, of which she now knows both the outcome and the necessity, but from which she suffered the tortures of the damned a few years ago, in making *Les Amants*.

In *Les Amants* Louis Malle asked Jeanne to do a scene regarded as the most scandalous and difficult in film today.

When the film was shot, Jeanne was involved in a passionate affair with Louis Malle.

The scene that Louis Malle asked Jeanne to play was the very scene she could not play without betraying him. It was he who asked it of her.

"I was ashamed and in love at the same time," she says. "I could not refuse to play the scene he wanted, because I loved him. And at the same time I knew that it was the end of our love. After asking me to do it, he could no longer stand to see me as others saw me, as he alone had seen me until then."

The affair dragged on interminably. For years Jeanne had to endure this tragic success.

She has not seen *Les Amants* again.

She regularly feels the temptation to call it quits, to be done with film. Usually this happens when a film is released.

"At that moment I feel like dropping everything and not starting up again. I am in the film that I made and the film is finished. I don't know where I am anymore."

"And then?"

"And then it starts all over again. I want to come back to life, and therefore I want to act. And suddenly I'm like a tree that seemed dead but really wasn't: buds pop out all over my body and in my head. Another film comes my way. Still more difficult than the last one. For one thing I've discovered is that if being an actress seemed hard at the beginning, with the passage of time and success it has become even more difficult, even more serious."

"Because the public expects more and more from you?"

"No. Because of the temptation—which you must fight against—to do whatever will please the public instead of what you really feel deeply is right. It becomes harder and harder to act, to make up your mind. In other words, to fight against the temptation of immodesty. To be an actress is not modest. If I say that it's natural for a woman to become an actress, one reason is that the profession presupposes an extraordinary desire for exhibitionism. You have to restrain that exhibitionism, and you have to be aware of it constantly. How many successful actresses can resist taking a part if they think it will enable them to display everything of which they are capable?"

"In other words, one should never choose a film solely because one is offered a juicy part."

"That's right. For an actress that is defeat: when she cannot resist showing herself in every scene of a lousy film. The film drags her down with it. When a building collapses, even if it is a building lived in by a king, the building wins: it will bury the king as surely as anyone else."

Has any man ever asked her to stop acting? No, that has never happened.

"That's something I can't even imagine. Anyway, you mustn't play games with words. When a man loves me, he loves the women that I am, with all her faults and qualities. He also loves the actress that I am, even if he doesn't admit it. He loves me partly because he's seen me in the movies. If I made him a gift of my freedom, he would love another woman, a woman who would no longer be me. No, if I tire of my profession sometimes, I do it alone, and because of the nature of the business."

She went off to Brittany. Returning by train, she wore a black dress, very beautiful, with a low-cut back. Her hair was the way she likes to wear it on vacation, down, soft, brushed like a little girl's hair. In Brittany she had been happy. She had been with Pierre. Pierre is Pierre Cardin.

Now he is coming to Mougins for the weekend, where she is

making a film with Jacques Demy. Mougins is near Nice. "Mother is there," she says, "and my little sister. Pierre comes down on weekends."

I remember. We were in a cafe in the place du Trocadéro. We met there before going to hear the Russian pianist [Sviatoslav] Richter. She told me about Pierre for the first time. Paris as yet knew nothing.

"I went to a fashion show, by chance. I saw him. It was love at first sight. I wanted to see him again, right away. I went back on the pretext of looking at some dresses. I knew about his reputation in Paris. I knew everything. It didn't matter at all. On the contrary. The obstacles, which I knew were real, attracted me all the more."

Jeanne is free. She anticipates prejudices and overcomes them. Before judging, before accepting that an obstacle is insuperable, she tries and she tries again.

She is free, and strong. Her stupefying strength is cloaked in extraordinary sweetness.

"I wanted Pierre to love me. I knew that he was capable of loving a woman. I had to be patient and gentle, and I had to be careful not to frighten him with the disgusting phantoms that sadistic society brandishes with pleasure. I had to make him understand that I could understand everything and accept everything and that he should, too."

Does this mean that she has escaped the loneliness that I mentioned earlier? "What a pleasure it would be to have another child!" she says. "To have a family of my own."

It's too soon to say. She is happy now: I know it, we all know it, all her friends, and, a little superstitiously perhaps, we don't want to announce anything before the time is ripe.

She is happy but for the shadow that recently stretched across the sky at Nice: the death of Roger Nimier. He had just killed himself on the same highway that Jeanne takes at night, in her Rolls, on her way back from Paris to Versailles. She had known him for a long time, ever since *Ascenseur pour l'échafaud*.

"Since Roger died," she says, "when I return to Paris I feel that I'm returning to an empty house, with the closets open and empty, a house that the people have just moved out of. Paris without Roger just isn't the same."

Jeanne. Jeanette, we call her. It's her real name, and she uses it.

Her real date of birth is the one she claims publicly: January 1928.

She is half English and half French but considers herself primarily French. She comes from Allier, an area that lies between the Loire and the Cher, where the Sioule flows through the gentle valleys that presage the more mountainous Auvergne. Her village is called Masirat. No one in Paris has ever heard of it.

"Thirty houses," she says. "You must come down some time. There are a lot of Moreaus—my relatives."

Two years ago she bought the most beautiful of the thirty houses for Anatole Désiré Moreau, her *enfant terrible* of a father, a headstrong man who made her childhood eventful as well as unusual and happy.

"When he drank, he would leave home, and someone would have to go at night and look for him in Montmartre, where he had a restaurant. We dragged him by his feet back to his room. Me on one foot, my little sister on the other, we pulled him up the stairs. How we would laugh!"

Anatole Désiré was not happy at first. Now he is. She had not even finished the Conservatory, she was nineteen years old, when the Comédie Française hired her to do Turgenev's *A Month in the Country*. "Why an actress?" Anatole Désiré asked himself. His wife had been a dancer. Why an actress rather than a dancer or a restaurateur like Michèle and himself?

"Because I liked the theater," says Jeanne. "I was crazy about the theater. I was crazy about watching other people act. And before long I wanted to change places with them, to leave the audience and get up on the stage and act. When you want to do theater because you love it, you love it all the more."

"Do you think there was a specifically female reason for your choice."

"Absolutely. Female and adolescent. It takes time for an adolescent to find himself or herself—time for a boy, an even longer time for a girl. Madame Bovary might have become an actress had she had the chance. I did have the chance."

"Was theater an escape?"

"No. Not for me. It was the opposite. The love that I experience in life, my anguish, my happiness—all that goes into my films, becomes an integral part of them. When I see a film that I've made, I recognize my life."

"Do you recognize yourself in all the films that you've made?"

"Yes. I can even say that I've liked every film I ever made except one: *Les Femmes marquées*. I agreed to do the film in order to pay my taxes, and I was punished for it. I had to shave off my hair. I felt really degraded when it was over. I agreed to do it in order to pay off my tax bill and not because I liked the film."

"How did you feel when you finished *Moderato Cantabile* and *Jules and Jim?*"

After *Moderato* I was dead, like the heroine. The same after *Jules and Jim*."

I saw Jeanne every day when she was making *Moderato*. Thus I know how conscientiously, how seriously she "internalizes" a role.

Shortly before shooting began, during the critical period when she has no choice but to leave her friends, she went to the little town near the mouth of the Gironde where the filming was to take place, a town called Blaye. A town notable for its bulrushes, wild ducks, sturgeon, and vineyards of white Graves.

"For a week I walked around Blaye until that little town was not only in my head but also in my feet. Gradually I became a citizen of Blaye."

She felt a constant need to know more about Anne Desbaresdes, the heroine she was supposed to embody. She was always asking me for more information about Anne's childhood and youth. She even wanted to know what Anne would have done in situations not mentioned in the script. One day I made up a background for her: "You were born near Limoges. Your father was a notary. You had three brothers. You had a lonely, dreamy childhood. One day, while hunting in Sologne, where you went every fall, you met your husband, Monsieur Desbaresdes. You were twenty years old." And so on. Jeanne was amazed. "That's it. Exactly right. Why didn't you tell me sooner?" I confessed, for her sake, to help her out, that I had invented it all on the spot.

We often repeat that story, which is one of the linchpins of our friendship, a part of our common memory.

What about when she isn't making a film? Then she becomes a free woman.

She walks.

She reads widely, with delirious pleasure. The last time I saw her she had just finished Scott Fitzgerald's *Tender Is the Night*. One day, on the telephone, she told me that she was making jam with Anna.

Another day she stayed in bed, sleeping, because she was upset.

She needs a lot of leisure, a lot of free time during the day. She needs to call Jérôme almost every day.

She can sleep at any time of the day or night, if she feels the need. At one in the afternoon, two in the afternoon, or all day long. Anna unplugs the telephone and closes the doors to the hallway leading up to the second floor.

"Mademoiselle is resting."

This need for deep oblivion stems not only from fatigue but also from ennui.

And then she begins working on a new film.

"I get up at six in the morning. I need to be completely alone. I'm always very afraid, but I know that no one can reassure me. I'm like a woman preparing for her wedding."

What could keep her from acting?

"Nothing, unless the theater and the cinema become so degraded that I can't see myself doing it anymore. Unless the only plays being put on are vulgar and the only films being made are commercial and terribly superficial. Then and only then would I lose heart. Anything else I can overcome. I've always overcome everything, even the torments that came from within. But the degradation of my profession I could not overcome."

Vogue, 1965

Margot Fonteyn

The apartment is a large one on the sixth floor of a building near the Seine. A maid closes the shutters. In the distance is the sound of Paris's morning rush hour. She has just called to say that she's on her way. She's making her way through the traffic, alone in the vast city that awaits her, with which she has a date tomorrow night.

There she is. Black and white. Black hair, white coat, black dress, black shoes. She is of average height. She excuses herself for being late. Her French is good. From the moment she enters and utters three words, her simplicity is evident: It is the great simplicity of Presence.

I look at her. I am in no hurry to ask her questions. We converse about unimportant things. Without haste. I am thinking about her as I sit in front of her. She knows it, and lets me go on thinking. Minutes pass. Eventually I notice that she, too, is looking at me. We're strangers, we say, and happy to make each other's acquaintance. There: "We've just smiled at each other, effortlessly, even though we were in no way obliged to. At the same moment both of us felt the need to smile. What has just developed between us is that unpredictable and marvelous thing, sympathy.

I've just forgotten that I came to see her in order to write an article about her. And she, too, has forgotten.

I tell her that we shall speak very little about dance. She laughs; she's glad to hear it. She says she hates to talk about dance. We understand each other quite well.

"A person dances, she does not talk about dance. Talking about dance has nothing to do with dancing, don't you agree?"

She gets up. She asks the maid to bring some tea. She walks across the room. She is very thin, almost tiny, and so youthful looking that age seems all at once a backward prejudice, an absurd, outdated notion, something familiar to our grandparents but no longer part of our lives. About her age, too, she talks comfortably. She makes the years vanish right from the start.

"You know, I am not nostalgic about the past, not even about my own past. Never, not even for a second, do I feel the desire to relive my younger days. I have forgotten my past. It doesn't interest me. We forget the things that don't interest us."

She hesitates, then adds: "I never regret the past, never. Even if I dream of the time when my husband was in good health, I do not regret that time."

"What would you call the strength that motivates you? Optimism? Or pessimism revised and corrected?"

"I don't know. I never thought of giving it a name. Is it important that it have a name?"

"No. Not at all."

She thinks about it anyway. She likes to "look at herself from outside," as she puts it.

"I have a kind of faith. I don't know what sort of faith it is. But it flows along with life. Whatever happens is for the best, I think."

"Even the worst?"

"Yes. What you have to do, I think, is find a way to make the best of the worst. Things may look bad, but there's some good in everything. The problem is to find it."

Hers is not an optimism like Candide's, a natural disposition to believe that "everything is for the best in the best of all possible worlds." No. Hers is a rare disposition: to live in the present.

"I'm very pleased to be alive now, to have been born in this modern age. To open a newspaper and read that yesterday men landed on the moon."

The same spirit that impels her to live *with* her times makes her approve of any action—however impassioned—that expresses love of life. She approves of today's youth, about whom she talks a great deal. She hopes that someone will teach the young people who have chosen the simple life about life's thousand treasures, that people will treat youth kindly and pay attention to its needs. She says that travel is essential, that spending money is essential, too, and that the only thing to do when one has money is to spend it. You have to discover what "comforts" are to your taste and then arrange to have them. Travel.

"You mustn't shut yourself up in a closed world, not even intellectually. My ideal is to be at home everywhere, in every place, in every environment. Our education, station, and snobbery tend to 'imprison' us in a world of our own and cut us off from life. I am against confining oneself to a narrow existence."

Any subject she takes up she takes seriously. She says nothing insincere. *This is no society matron.* It's remarkably reassuring to discover this. Her thin, triangular face speaks as a whole, smiles as a whole. There is nothing tentative about her smile. When it comes, it inundates her face. I stare excitedly at her.

"Who are you?"

"I am the wife of Roberto Arias."

"A dancer?"

"Yes. But before, this dancer did not know who she was. Now she knows: she is the wife of Roberto Arias. The miracle for me is that this man exists."

As everyone knows, this man, whom she met relatively late in life, at age 35, and married in 1955, was wounded in Panama in 1964 and subsequently lost the power to move or even speak— for months. She speaks of this calmly, as if speaking of something that she has thought over *fully.* I don't dare ask for news of Roberto Arias. She guesses this. She smiles, smiles again, and then laughs.

"He is better. He has resumed his position in the legislature. He is able to hold a cigar, provided it's a very good Havana cigar, and a glass of champagne. His speech is improved."

I cannot keep from looking at her steely legs. The genius hidden in those legs also saved her from what she refuses to call "the tragedy." She was forced to work even after Roberto Arias's accident, during the time when he was suffering from a terrifying meningitis.

"I am lucky," she says. "It must be harder for the others, much harder. I was obliged to forget him for an hour and a half every day, you see. Because dance is not something you can do without thinking about it. The concentration that the profession requires is enormously helpful when it comes to withstanding hard blows. After I finished dancing, I went back to him, fortified."

With all their might they've both put the tragedy behind them.

"If you don't want tragedy, you don't have it. It can come into your life only if you open the door."

They spent last summer at the seacoast. She insisted that Roberto swim, with the help of his son, stretched out on an inflatable raft. They were afraid they might lose hold, but he said, "Don't worry. Paralyzed people always float—that's one advantage of the situation."

The miracle is that he is so alive and so able to mock "the accident."

Before she met Roberto, she says, she had no idea that a woman could so fuse with a man, or lose her freedom with such joy.

"What does freedom mean in such a case? I don't even think about it. You appear to be two people, but that's just an illusion. A woman cannot know who she is until she knows who her husband is. I made my way all alone, not knowing who I was. I was nailed in a box by success until the day I met him."

"What is success?"

She searches for a way to say it.

"The smoke of the cigarette you're smoking now."

This territory, unknown to billions of men and women, is territory that she knew so young—at age fifteen—that to her it is no longer the territory of adventure but her native country. Dance defines her but in the same way as another woman might be defined by her profession. Ultimately we share a common fate.

"After forty-two minutes of curtain calls, do you feel as lonely as ever?"

"More than ever," she says. "The superstition about success is so great that as soon as you have it and other people do not, you no longer have the right to complain. Deprived of the right to speak, solitude grows, digs in, becomes hateful. Until one night Roberto Arias knocks on the door of your dressing room—at the Metropolitan Opera in New York—to remind you that you had known each other in college. That was seventeen years ago."

"He guessed?"

"He guesses everything."

She had fallen for him when she was eighteen, at first sight. And the minute she recognized him, she fell again. Except for that bullet in the spine—would I dare speak those words? No.

Little by little I grasped what was responsible for her second career, for the second wind that, from the time of her meeting Nureyev at age forty-three, propelled her onto the international scene for a second time: her passionate desire to hold fate at bay. Or, to put it another way, a taste for the ultimate adventure. She chose to dance with Nureyev precisely because he was so young, just twenty-one, so strong, and so extraordinary in his virtuosity.

"I love a challenge. I told myself that he would obliterate me. I had a choice: to dance with him or not. I chose to make the effort. To make the effort that I would have to make in order not to lose face with him or because of him."

It worked. In capital after capital, to thunderous applause, they danced together with deep mutual understanding. And he, too, when he dances with her, must make an effort: to adapt himself to the uniquely graceful way in which her body moves.

"We get along quite well. We think alike about dance. We're both serious in the same way."

What does she mean by serious?

"Hard work and being hard on yourself. And never letting success go to your head."

"Have you ever?"

"When I was very young, yes, for a few months. But I soon realized that my friends were deserting me, and I saw that I had gone off in the wrong direction."

Nureyev is as alone as she was before she met the man from Panama. She understands him. She accepts his dissipated life. She feels friendship and respect for him. His crises—he can be very difficult—are always justified, in her view. They stem from a knowledge of dance the likes of which she has never encountered in anyone else.

Having achieved the highest rank in the Royal Ballet some fifteen years ago, she is now a Permanent Guest of that company—in order to make room for others. She explains this in great detail. But the outward symbols of her success bore her.

Tomorrow she is dancing. She will give four performances with Nureyev at the Paris Opera. Four performances before an audience unlike the New York or the London audience in that it can show enormous enthusiasm one year and none the next, merely because fashions have changed.

"I've never suffered that fate in Paris," she says, "but I know that it can happen."

Thus while she likes a challenge she has no illusions about the future. She looks forward to it. On the surface it will be what it will be, but in reality it will be whatever she makes of it.

Vogue, 1968

Leontyne Price

She is very beautiful, as fresh as a mermaid emerging from the sea, with deliciously dark skin, gleaming, as golden as if she had just returned from a summer in the Islands. She is not fat but abundant. Her flesh is light: tender and slightly puffed like an infant's. The minute she opens her mouth, the minute she *speaks*, you realize that this flesh was needed *around* the voice, to nourish it as the good earth nourishes its fruit, so that it might achieve its full depth, its marvelous velvet sound.

Her first words, her speaking voice, suggest the other voice. The room resounds with surprising, distant harmonies. La Voce streams from her body as from a conch. We are inside a seashell. Even speaking she is already singing.

"The minute I wake up, even before I start to talk, I feel immediately, in the depths of my body, how *it* is. If *it* is as it should be, that is *la felicità.*"

It? La Voce. And she adds, in the language of Verdi: "La Voce è la felicità."

"Sublime black monster," say the newspapers. And in the

packed Théâtre des Champs-Elysées I heard someone in the en-
thusiastic crowd say this: "Even Callas never sang the great aria
in *Tosca* like that!"

She heard it, too. She bows simply, naturally. She knows. Anything that one can say about her voice, she knows: that she is the
repository of a treasure, and that she is at the point in her career
where, in the prize ring of international opera, she is the number
one contender.

"For two years I have been in *securità*. La Voce is readier than
ever. I feel that my voice is coming into its maturity."

Who is the bearer of that voice, Leontyne Price?

I think I know now that she and her voice cannot be separated.
They are one and the same.

If the question is phrased differently—What is the relationship between Leontyne Price and the gift that is in her?—it has
an answer of sorts. That relationship is, I think, an extraordinary
one, compounded of fear, anger, and love.

First of all fear. A certain kind of fear. That such a fantastic gift
was bestowed upon her, a little black girl from Mississippi, that
she was obliged to suffer this fate, is frightening. A duty was imposed upon her: to develop a rare artistic gift to the full and carry
it around the world. And she has only one lifetime to do it in:
her own.

Whence a certain anger. No other word will do.

She levels a finger of accusation. She accuses La Voce. No children because of La Voce. No marriage because of La Voce. No
personal life because of La Voce. She must give it her all: all her
time, all her energy, all her emotions, her entire life. Everything.

"I will never be a whole woman. With each success I am more
certain of that than ever. I know that success is what I must accept in place of a personal life. *It is the most difficult thing in the
world to accept.*"

After a silence she adds: "Without God it would not be possible. Without God nothing is possible. I cannot function without
this constant belief."

Her only solace: the love of God. Solely responsible and only
solace: God is both. The love of music, hence the love of God,
hence the love of nature. Including nature's forbidden parts: the
soft cotton fields of Mississippi where she might have loved a
man and listened to her children laugh.

Leontyne Price's faith comes to her from the South, the legacy of her black father and mother. She is a simple, absolute woman.

No sooner does she point the finger of accusation at La Voce and at the feverish pace of a life lived in all the capitals of opera— Milan, Moscow, London, and so forth—than she remembers that God willed La Voce and that He must be obeyed.

And when she thinks of God, she thinks immediately afterward of her father and mother back in Laurel, through whom the divine will passed. When she speaks of them, which she does as a child of fifteen might speak of her parents, one comes closest to what is most essential in her, most protected from La Voce. She loves her parents more than anything else.

Oddly, it is as though her happiness or unhappiness still depended on them. It is almost as if she is still sorry for having left her home in Laurel.

"My parents are simple, quiet, happy people. Whenever I go to see them, I come away stronger than before."

There is no doubt: her parents have become her children. The children she does not have. She would like them to live forever. She crosses herself when she says that they are in good health and still strong.

Apart from that unchanged love of a child for her parents, what other love has there been in her life?

"I have not been without love," she says. "I was married once. But I don't want to talk about it."

The marriage must have been while she was doing *Porgy and Bess* on Broadway. "I have not been without love": The negative is terrifying; it reveals her privation.

When Herbert von Karajan heard her sing "Pace, pace mio Dio" [from Verdi's *La Forza del Destino*—Trans.] at Carnegie Hall in 1955, he hired her on the spot to come to Vienna. At the Metropolitan Opera in 1961, after *Il Trovatore*, the audience gave her an ovation that lasted forty-two minutes; then and there her stunning martyrdom began. Now her only affair is with a faceless and nameless partner, a partner that adores her and jealously seeks to keep her for itself: the public.

"It is a great challenge. A great thing, the public. But because of it I've probably given up many very important things."

She doesn't say what they are.

She is not a proud woman. Her simplicity is of the kind that one finds among the great. She accepts herself as she is, for better or worse.

"I am a black American woman. I represent my race and my country. I must strive constantly to do better so that I can represent them better."

She speaks of her race with emotion.

"I am proud of being black."

She speaks of the growing suffering of her race, but also of its hopes and its progress.

"You can say that we're no longer asking. We're demanding. It had to happen."

Previous black singers had limited themselves to jazz. Now they are beginning to make opera their own. After Marian Anderson came Grace Bumbry and herself, Leontyne Price.

The newspapers say that she is just as beautiful as she was seven years ago when she made her debut in *Il Trovatore* at the Metropolitan. Miraculously unchanged, they say. Why?

Suddenly I understand. It is a young girl of forty who stands before me.

Decorously clad in a black gown. Around her neck, fine pearls. Over the heart, a pin. She can't be more than twenty-five or thirty. No, they tell me. No. Tomorrow is her fortieth birthday. It's possible. But as far as the feelings are concerned, the imprisoned youth remains intact. That is the most obvious thing about her. La Voce and the fabulous care that she has had to take of her voice from the days when she was still playing with dolls have protected her from any withering of the heart. And when she laughs—for there is gaiety in her, too, ready to take flight— her youth explodes, heartrending and superb.

Vogue, 1968

Madeleine Renaud Has Genius

One night I waited for her in her dressing room. The audience was still applauding when she came in and walked straight toward me.

"Touch my heart."

Her heart was beating wildly. Her hands were frozen. When the curtain comes down, it's a dead woman who takes her bows, says Marcabru. Her face was dead. I moved away from her. She was unapproachable. When she leaves the stage it is several minutes before she comes back to life, before she becomes recognizable—even to herself. I waited until she had dressed and the last admirers had gone.

Then I pulled her toward me and asked, "How do you do it?"

She thought about it for a moment.

"I forget everything."

"Is that it?"

"Yes. That's it."

Another day I asked her how she felt when people said she had genius.

"I'd very much like to feel immensely proud," she says, "but no, it has no effect on me. I don't know what genius is in an actor. What does have an effect on me is the ability to make people forget about Madeleine, completely, the ability to turn myself inside out."

"You do make people forget her."

"Really? Then I'm doing well."

Beckett told me once that "she has genius, she has intelligence written all over her, on her skin, everywhere."

She tells me this: genius begins with pain. Between the moment when a character first takes possession of an actor and the moment when the actor projects that character on the stage is a time of terror. During that period Jean-Louis Barrault creates around her a magic circle like the one that is traced around the savage warriors in certain tribal rituals. No one is allowed to come near her. She feels as if she had been skinned alive. Jean-Louis speaks to her with utmost gentleness.

"If Jean-Louis touched me during that time," she says, "I would scream with pain."

The torture lasts two weeks. Madeleine feels anxious, sleeps little, doesn't eat, and loses weight. She can only wait. The miracle has never yet failed to happen, but that doesn't lessen the fear that some time it won't. When the pain stops, when the quest is over, Madeleine steps outside the circle. The character took possession of her, of course, only when she had ceased to expect it.

"Sometimes a small detail is all it takes. For the Lady of the Trees [in Marguerite Duras's play *Des journées entières dans les arbres*—Trans.] it was the hat. I put on the Saint Laurent hat and it happened. By the time you get to rehearsal, a lot of work has already been done. For your Lady, for instance, I spent the whole summer watching elderly women—how they walked, what shoes they wore: such things are important."

I always have the same question: How do you do it?

I don't ask it anymore. It's pointless. She can't answer. She doesn't know. She remains innocent in her own eyes. I prefer to look at her, to listen to her speak about other things, having to do with the theater and with what people say about the theater.

I look at her carefully, and I listen. I see that she is kind, that her celebrated smile is indeed beautiful, and that her gaze is sharp, perhaps even luminous. But I also see—and is there anyone who has worked with her who has not seen?—I also see that a savage power is sovereign over Madeleine and that she stands ready, if need be, to heed the most primitive injunctions with exemplary docility.

Marcabru said, speaking of her, that she is the very innocence of tragedy. The words moved her greatly. One might also say that she is tragedy in a barbarous if well-bred age. She thanks us, she is eager to "serve us well," and she has played Marivaux to perfection, but all the while she was awaiting her turn to speak. And now she does speak. She began some years ago, at dusk. And now, in the sunset of youth, she shouts at the top of her lungs.

They say she plays the women in Beckett, Billetdoux, and Duras. But what does that mean?

Isn't the truth that she seized those women, dragged them off to her lair, and devoured them?

That with patience and frenzy she poisoned herself with them, until she no longer knew whether it was she or they who felt pain or happiness?

What remains of our blanched books? Not a word that she has not invented.

I had no desire to discuss with her the woman to whom she refers as the Lady of the Trees. But patiently she waited until I was in a mood to say something—this happened about midway through the series of rehearsals—and in a frenzy she said: "Tell me a little about what this person was like? She was your mother, no doubt. Tell me."

"Yes."

She wanted to see photographs. I showed her one, of a young woman. And I gave her some details—external details about the character. The woman was the daughter of farmers from the Pas-de-Calais. She taught in a school for natives [in Vietnam, then a French colony—Trans.]. She was a little captain of primary education. Jules Ferry was her master.*

"What else? What kind of dresses did she wear?"

---

*Jules Ferry is the government minister who established the system of public national education in France—Trans.

"Not dresses. Sacks. She wasn't flirtatious. In her old age she became bitter. She didn't want to accept the fact that she had trained hundreds of other captains who were fighting for their country's freedom. She refused to remember. She wanted to maintain her despair intact."

"What else?"

"Of her three children she preferred the eldest, a son, proud, affectionate, and a ne'er-do-well."

"Ah, yes, I see. Was he always her favorite?"

"Always."

"Thank you."

She never brought up the subject again. She saw Yves Saint Laurent. She saw him repeatedly. She spoke little. At that time she was plunged into suffering, from which she had little respite. And then it passed.

And then, one day, I arrived at the Odéon for a dress rehearsal and at the door of the theater I stopped dead in my tracks. My mother was on stage at the Odéon.

Madeleine, who is round, young in body, and alert, had become emaciated, ancient, wasted. Madeleine, a true Parisian, had just made an inspection tour of the primary schools in the Plain of Reeds, traveling by oxcart. And her Sunday dress, taken from the closet—a sack—I recognized it.

"How do you do it?"

"I have no shame. That is essential. If I'm asked to lift my skirts up to my elbows, I do it. You mustn't have any shame."

"I'd like to write a comic play for you, about women. You would play ten different women. There wouldn't be any men."

She explodes with joy.

"Ah, what a muddle there is in women! What extraordinary plays you could write with that muddle! An actress must use the muddle. She mustn't make it disappear. On the contrary."

For a brief moment she dreamed about herself.

"You didn't know me. I was full of contradictions. So many things accumulate in old people. The years pile up. If you're too young, you haven't enough weight to play a character like the Lady of the Trees. And if you're too old, you haven't the strength. It's very tiring to play with all the baggage you have to carry around, all the weight that the years pile up."

She is lucky, she says, because in every decade she managed to find work suited to her physical age. But not until she was thirty-five. Until then she remained an ingenue—so much so that they didn't know what roles to give her at the Comédie Française.

"When you start in the theater you need to nourish yourself with the classics, but soon you must move on to the contemporary theater. Only there are too few contemporary playwrights. Of the five new plays that will open [in Paris] this February, not one is French. Yet I'm amazed by the number of good actors in France—a stellar array."

What does she think of film? Not a great deal, because it's much easier than the stage.

"The theater is a terrible thing. You never get used to it." The fear is total. Before a performance she locks herself alone in her dressing room for two hours. What does she do? Or, rather, what happens during those two hours? She prepares for a journey. She prepares to drop everything and go as far away as possible—inside the theater: that, after all, is pure wandering. Where is the hole in which she was spinning fantasies on the night when Beckett gave the starting signal? In Ireland? In some desert? And this gaze upon her grown child dancing the samba—where is its frontier?

Vogue, 1966

Melina

Is Melina Mercouri as tall as she seems? Perhaps not.

Her hips are narrow, her shoulders broad, her legs and arms no doubt too long, her head perched high. Her movement is always graceful, magnificent.

A superb woman? More: a superb creature.

The golden rule for a woman this tall is extravagance mysteriously distributed from head to toe. The first time you see her, you're struck by this. And whenever you see her after that, your emotion at first gazing upon a woman of such royal bearing is reawakened.

She is beautiful in the manner of a young athlete. Perfection of form is very likely an androgynous quality. Only in the human arena does one discriminate. In Melina's case I do not discriminate. She is a beauty without boundaries, for beauty is a quality that can be possessed by any living thing: a horse, a tree, a woman.

Blond. From beneath the mane admirable yellow eyes stare at you. Her mouth is as it should be: large. She is barefoot and dressed, as she almost always is, in a man's shirt and trousers. Her wild hair hangs in her eyes. She sits not like everyone else but with her feet tucked up under her. Or else she stretches out. She seems always to have just come from where? From running in the hills or along the beach, never from the city.

There are people she likes and people she doesn't like. Once you get past these categories, she loves all humanity, and she loves Greece, Paris, and the stage.

Lewis Carroll distinguishes between happy laughter and amused laughter. In Melina's eyes there is happy laughter. Her smile is extraordinarily tender. With her, amused laughter can assume fantastic proportions. Melina's mad laughter explodes without regard for either place or company. No matter where or in what circumstances, Melina's laughter will carry Melina away. She is helpless before its force.

"She isn't 'presentable,'" says [Jules] Dassin. In the world of officialdom she is very unhappy and when she is unhappy she plays her part very badly.

When you know her, you are reluctant to speak of her in terms of defects and qualities. You are tempted to go straight to her deeper nature.

In Melina, character in the strict sense—harmony between the individual and his or her environment—seems unimportant. Between Melina's nature and the outside world there is apparently nothing. She does not lend herself to psychological dissection. Either she is there, whole, before your eyes or she is not there at all. Dissimulation, accommodation, compromise: she doesn't know the meaning of the words.

Melina's nature is among the most beautiful that I have been privileged to know. It results from a marriage of generosity with intelligence. She is deeply loved by many people. The sympathy that she evokes transcends her person: "You're simply happy that people like Melina exist. As you seek the sun, you seek Melina. You seek out intelligence when it welcomes you with open arms. You feel good when you're with her, when you're with this woman-who-has-no-home because wherever she is is made Home by the force of her presence.

"To be at home: what does that mean to you?"

"I don't know. In my life I don't understand what that means. 'At home' is people, not a place. When I'm with people with whom I can relax and say whatever is on my mind, I'm at home."

"What things do you find it possible to miss?"

"The ocean. But other than that, nothing. I detest the idea of 'home, sweet home.' I really despise it."

"You have nothing of your own?"

"Nothing. What I'm proudest of is that I own nothing. That's a terrible thing to be proud of, isn't it? The idea that one can do without ownership in a world where everyone wants nothing else. Once I owned a car, which I bought with what I earned in Greece. Everybody in Athens drove that car except me."

"If you go on spending everything you make, what will become of you later on?"

"I'll never be homeless. My friends tell me, 'Don't worry, there will always be a room for you in our home.' I'm sure I'll always have a place to go, and that's all I need."

She doesn't notice the decor in the places where she stays. She's totally incapable of it, she says. On the stage or in a film she's aware of the set, but not in people's homes.

"It doesn't matter where I am as long as I'm with someone I like. The only time I want to be alone is when I'm sick, but I still want people to be waiting on the other side of the door."

Since meeting Jules Dassin she has lived in that luxurious no-man's-land of grand hotels serving an international clientele. As long as there are comfortable bathrooms and sofas, all the rest—especially the "beautiful objects" beloved by women of the indoor breed—can disappear from the face of the earth.

"I can't accept solitude," Melina says. "Solitude is terribly selfish. If you're a genius, you can be alone. Otherwise, you're like everybody else and solitude is a weakness."

She adds, smiling, that even a person who doesn't like solitude can still be "rather secretive."

In this regal nonchalance, this scorn for possession and dissimulation, there is a violent and mysterious gift for freedom. It is as though freedom for Melina means not only casting off ties but also creating another order of possession. To possess nothing is to possess that which cannot be possessed in singular or concrete form.

To possess nothing is to possess Athens, the sea, love, and happiness, as well as pure despair.

That is Melina: citizen of the sea, citizen of liberty.

Around her walls have fallen. She stands naked in the midst of her world. Melina is a metaphysical tramp. She is also Modern Tragedy, which does not wear ancient robes, as all too many people believe, but is, as we can see with disturbing clarity, tragic nonetheless. I am the woman you see in front of you, Melina says. Take her or leave her. I will do nothing to please you that I wouldn't do anyway, even if you expected nothing from me. And that way I will please you all the more.

Ten Thirty, Summer

She is forty years old.

She is forty in the film that Dassin has just finished: *Ten Thirty, Summer.*

I think—in fact I'm sure—that she has modeled the role of Maria closely on what she is in real life, body and soul.

She is Maria. Her husband (Peter Finch) is Paul. Their young and tender friend (Romy Schneider) is Claire.

Time takes its toll of any love, and Maria's and Paul's is no different. With calm desperation Maria accepts the inevitable failure, old age, the end of her love, the end of everything. She does not struggle. She drinks. For Maria lives the end of her love affair as fully as the beginning, with the same interest and the same passion she felt at the outset. In order to be equal to that terrifying event, the end of the affair, Maria must drink, and she does drink. She watches herself sink. Maria looks on at Maria's inevitable foundering. In a cool and dignified manner.

Yet she does something to alter fate. Or, rather, fate offers her a chance, and she grabs it.

Paul and Claire have for some time been attracted to each other without knowing it, but Maria has been aware of it for months. Also developing for some time is a love that dares not speak its name, though Maria has known about it, too, for months. Who is to blame when feelings change? Nobody. What can be done about it? Love must not be impeded, for loving is still the best way of living in this world. Should nothing be done, then, even if doing nothing causes suffering? Yes. But there is a way to make that suffering bearable: by bringing it upon oneself. If Maria spoke of such things, she would say to Paul: I shall give you Claire, I shall give you a second woman, and in that way I shall participate in your love. That love will have an author: me.

Maria invites Claire to spend her vacation in Spain with her and Paul. In the promiscuity of summer hidden feelings become known, burst forth into the light of day, and desire declares itself openly. The deed will be done.

Such triangles are known by a clichéd term, and usually condemned. Ménages à trois often seem hateful to those who look at them. For love is still conceived in medieval terms: it is supposed to be absolute and eternal, like faith. To declare one's love is implicitly to declare that one will love forever. Will there ever come a time when we will say: "For the moment it's you that I love," or "I am in love, and right now you're the one"? Perhaps not.

Disorder reigns in the hotel, in souls, in feelings, and in the sunless city where the young criminal Rodrigo Paestra is hiding.

Abetted by this disorder, Paul and Claire exchange their first kiss, on a balcony at the end of a corridor. Meanwhile, from another balcony, Maria is watching them, watching her bitter, terrifying triumph. And in the same moment, in the precise same instant, she also sees a human shape wrapped in a brown blanket at the base of a chimney: Rodrigo Paestra, who expects to be trapped like a rat come dawn.

Maria leaves the hotel and saves—or thinks she is saving—Paestra by taking him to a field a few miles outside the town.

The next day, when she comes to get him and take him away, she finds him dead. He has killed himself during the night. He died of love, without a word, refusing or finding himself unable to give any explanation, contemptuous of explanation of any kind.

A heavy cloud hangs over the day following this discovery. When Maria falls into a drunken sleep, Claire and Paul become lovers. Maria is delirious. Fleeing across Spain with Paestra, sharing a common danger, might have miraculously resurrected their old love. But Paestra, playing his hand badly, killed himself. Nothing left to be done? No. Nothing.

Claire understands what Maria wanted. She understands the

contradiction in Maria's position: that after having "given" Claire to Paul, she wants to take Paul back. But Claire has begun to love Paul and insolently awaits her moment.

And on that very night Maria gives it to her, in Madrid. In Paestra's despair Maria has recognized the lost paradise of passionate love. Next to which their problems seem trivial. Suddenly everything becomes clear. Adultery has its charm only when it violates a taboo, even if that taboo is illusory. When the taboo is removed, adultery loses its charm. Maria removes the taboo against adultery: the two lovers may do what they like, for she has withdrawn from the game. In Madrid of a summer's night Maria finds herself plunged into a dreadful yet superb solitude. Has she suffered an upsetting defeat? Or won a victory?

For what will the others become without her? We do not know.

Vogue, 1966

Sylvie and Her Phantoms

Sylvie [1883–1970, real name Thérèse Sylvie—Trans.] was a leading French actress, a star of stage and screen. The best known of her films is *La Vieille Dame indigne* by René Allio.

Q. You must be mistaken. You can't be eighty-three years old.

A. Shall I send for my birth certificate?

Q. Maybe you should. I really mean it.

A. I can't believe it myself, you know, but it seems to be true. All you reporters tell me so. They asked me what diet I follow, and I told them the Blédine for the elderly. Next time I'll say I'm a hundred years old.

Q. What is your secret?

A. I don't know. I don't understand a thing about it. I've never done anything special. I watch my weight, because when I gain weight my nose follows my stomach: It gets fat. That's all. But listen, I'm not about to start taking myself seriously now. I've never done that. But tell me, what's to become of me now? What should I do? Will you tell me that?

Q. Theater?

A. No! That's finished! I mean, I'll soon be leaving for America, and I'm going to play Agnes over there, start a new career. But what else can I do? I made my debut in the role of little Joas in *Athalie*, and I ended by playing Athalie. I've come full circle, you see.

With Father Antoine

Q. Do you get many offers of roles?

A. I don't want to act anymore, I tell you. That's over, and it's a good thing. What roles do you want me to do? What could you as a director offer me that I could stand and that could stand me? I can't act on a chalk mark with my eyes on a prompter. I was brought up by Father Antoine. You had to walk down the staircase looking at the audience and turn right at the ramp. "At the ramp, Madame": that was my career. With Father Antoine you had to go down to your place in a straightforward motion, not sideways like a crab. In theater you've got to split in two, forget everything, lose yourself. That's the way I acted.

Q. What actors do you like?

A. I like Fresnay. I like the way he captures a character. Moreau is good. I like Loleh Bellon. Bellon is very good! Bardot is intelligent. She's been at it for ten years, you know.

Q. Lucienne Bogaerth?

A. Wonderful but lazy. It's her own fault.

One Fine Morning

Q. Did you ever stop doing theater?

A. (Speaking very softly.) Never. But I don't enjoy it for myself any more. I go to the theater, I like to go, but it's not for me. The stage grabbed me, you know, when I was sixteen. I probably liked it.

Q. Probably?

A. Because I stuck with it, you see. I liked being anybody but myself. But I'm not sure that I could—that I could have been a middle-class housewife with children.

Q. If there is a crisis in the French theater, what is the reason for it, in your opinion?

A. No playwrights.

Q. And direction?

A. Generally speaking, there's too much direction for my taste. It's confused, it's all over the place, you run after it, it's not constrained, it doesn't encompass my characters. But still, there's Peter Brook, there's Roger Blin, there's Jean-Louis Barrault. There's Jean Vilar: hats off to Jean Vilar. And there are others.

Q. What do you do all day?

A. What do I do all day? Can you tell me? You know, I was born the way I am and I'll die that way. I don't know what I do with the day.

Q. Where are you from?

A. From Paris, from the Thirteenth Arrondissement. From over by the place Jeanne-d'Arc. Every once in a while I go over there, and not much has changed. My father worked on the barges, "sur les chalands qui passent." My mother was a school-teacher. She was an angel.

Q. Were you bored?

A. You know, it's funny, I take after my mother, I'm always bored. When I'm bored, I take after her. When I'm gone for good, I don't know if I'll see her again—all that's tittle-tattle—but I tell myself maybe, just maybe, I will see her. When something good happens in your life you instinctively seek out some person, and for me, she was that person. I never had a great love in my love. I had only her. She was my child. If she were still alive she'd be more than a hundred years old, but that doesn't matter. She died in 1924, and I never got over it.

Q. You knew that one day you would lose her.

A. No, I didn't know. That's why I never had children. She was the only love of my life, and her death was my great sorrow. The great memory of my adolescence is of my mother's face when I told her that I had won first prize for acting and that I'd been awarded a medal. That and nothing else.

Q. Do you see any difference between age sixty and age eighty?

A. None. I didn't know anything was happening. Would you believe me if I told you that I'm more active now than when I was thirty? Senility must be settling in, I'm behaving as if I were a child again. I've become talkative, curious, and an avid eater, which I never used to be. Can you tell me what I'm made of? I go to my doctor and he sends me away. Nothing wrong with me. But one fine morning, you know, something will go click. That's the way I want it. Pleasant, no?

When the Mood Strikes

Q. Do you go out every day?

A. Of course. I ride horseback. That's what I like to do.

Q. You must have a secret. Otherwise you couldn't do such things.

A. I don't keep regular hours. Do you think that's it?

Q. Who knows?

A. When the mood strikes, I open my shutters. If the weather's bad, I go back to bed. I eat when I please and go to bed when I please. I have no set hours. I've never done anything in a set way. Why make plans? You're making me talk about myself, but do I really know anything about myself? I don't think so. All that I know is that I never bore myself. I was good at playing lots of other people but not myself. I was even Jeanne d'Albret in a successful play. It was by Bourdet, but it was good.

Q. Do you receive guests? Do you give dinner parties?

A. No. I don't know how to give dinners. I don't know how to receive guests. I don't know how to do much of anything. I try to sew, for instance. I cut out the pattern, but then I can't fit the pieces together. I invite people out to a little Greek restaurant called Samarkos in the place de l'Odéon. Check everything I've told you. Look it all over, my dear young lady. I'm counting on you to make sure that any slips I may have made don't interfere with my future career.

Q. Your career where?

A. On the moon.

Q. Do you have many friends?

A. Not many. I have pals. I don't know where friendship begins or ends. If I'm in distress, I don't wake anybody up to tell them about it. So . . .

Q. What can do an actor the most harm?

A. Lack of talent.

Q. Don't make fun. I meant the question seriously. Is appearing in a string of bad plays or films the worst thing that can happen to an actor?

A. No. You can make thirty bad films. If you hit upon a good role in the thirty-first, it's a fresh start and you're on your way.

A Stroke of Luck

Q. Are the people you see of your own age?

A. No. People my age are all nailed to their chairs by rheumatism.

Q. You don't have any rheumatism?

A. None at all! Imagine that! A stroke of luck, I don't know why. The only thing wrong with me is occasional indigestion. I eat too much. I miss some of the people who've died: Father Antoine, Bourdet, Camus. Camus wrote: "Make haste to enjoy yourself, gather your happiness quickly, for in its shadow pain and death grow side by side." That's in *Le Chevalier d'Olmedo* [by Lupe de Vega, translated into French by Camus—Trans.], which I did at the Avignon festival.

Q. Which of the films and plays in which you've performed recently are your favorites?

A. On stage, *La Visite de la vieille dame.* In film, *Les Anges du péché*—that was 1940, it's old, but write it down anyway. Most recently is *La Vieille Dame indigne* and her twin Lady Hodwin in *Belphégor.* I've been very spoiled by life. I'm able to stop working, you know.

Q. Tell me about *La Vieille Dame indigne,* which you've just made with René Allio.

A. We shot the film at L'Estaque. We rented a wonderful little house where we were happy as all get out. We'd been living in Le Corbusier's Cité heureuse or radieuse, I can't remember which, and then we went to shoot the film at L'Estaque, we went to Toulon, we went to the races. It was the good life. We got on very well. René Allio is wonderful.

Q. Give me a snapshot description of Madame Berthe—

if Brecht didn't invent her.* A snapshot of her in her youth
as well.

A. The picture of her youth is taken from a classic: *Marie-
Jeanne, or the Woman of the People,* which is from before 1913,
before anybody was born. Isn't that a nice title? But you've
never heard of this classic. You've never heard of anything.

Q. When are you entirely serious?

A. When I go looking for Mother. Then it's all over. I close the
shutters. It's over, the shutters are closed.

Le Nouvel Observateur, 1965

*The film is based on a story by Brecht—Trans.

Queen Bardot

Even if they wished to ignore her, they wouldn't be able to. Everyone, from Cardinal Spellman to General de Gaulle, recognizes her at a glance. She can be talked about any day of the week. No need to look for a topical occasion. She is now in the flesh. She is France today in the eyes of moviegoers around the world.

She is twenty-four years old. She is the most famous movie star in the world. She makes a hundred million per film these days. She happens to be French. She had to come from somewhere. For her it happens to be France.

A French girl, then, she penetrates the hearts and bodies of moviegoers everywhere, now with the face of a lovely little delinquent from Belleville, now with the honey eyes of a country lass from the Touraine. She is famous even in Japan. (Come to think of it, what do they know about her in the people's democracies?) From Japan to New York and vice versa, she represents the unavowed aspiration of the male human being, his potential infidelity—and infidelity of a very special kind, which would lead him to the opposite of his wife, to the "woman of wax" whom he could model at will, make and unmake in any way he wished, even unto death.

We shall call her by her real name: Queen Bardot.

Many women don't like her. She doesn't look them in the eye. They look at her with disapproval, rather taken aback with fright. I'm sorry to have to say this about my sisters, but it's one of the reasons this article was written. Women see her as woman become calamity, which descends upon a man as might a maelstrom. This calamity is all the more awesome for being natural, and they, who traditionally regard themselves as doing their men good, can't compare.

Driven from the home by these women, denied though she may be, Queen Bardot comes galloping back at full tilt, like nature herself. In France especially, where her threat is closest at hand, there is not a single drawing room—be it in Paris or Dijon—where she has not been discussed on one or more occasions. And discussed, perhaps, as though she were a natural disaster, like a flood or a storm.

Until a few weeks ago women who didn't like her had plenty of ammunition to use against her. Since *En cas de malheur*, the number of such women is considerably diminished. The worst has happened: Queen Bardot plays her role *as no one else could*, with the perfection of miraculous coincidence. So people say: as if she were actually there. Of course. It's true. Straight from the place de la Mairie at Saint-Tropez, Bardot has climbed up on the screen. Or, if you prefer, she's climbed down from the screen into the street with us. In *Les Bijoutiers du clair de lune* she was bored with herself. In *En cas de malheur* she is happy to be Bardot—like a cat with her kittens—splendid, satisfied, finally at one with her celebrity. I feel sorry for anyone who did not like *En cas de malheur*. I was delighted with the film, delighted that Queen Bardot exists, delighted with her victory over me—who had until then been suspicious of her as of a plague that might turn out to be something else: false, fraudulent, and fashionable. How pleased I was that the plague turned out to be real!

Only she has survived the "wave" that she was riding, along with others historically associated with her. She has now transcended the influence of that wave. When Françoise Sagan, in one of her excellent interviews, said of her generation that it was more intelligent than the preceding one (shrewder, I think, would have come closer to the mark, but perhaps that's because I'm getting on in years), it might have seemed that Queen Bardot was actually excluded from that wave. That her feet were dry. Others make their way, in their wave, with recognizable merits of one degree or another. She alone thrusts forward like a loco-motive of history—the history of women or of the cinema, which-ever you prefer. She is beyond mere talent or pleasantness. She makes such criteria meaningless. Of the others one can always think that as time passes they will change somehow. With Bardot's power, however, there's no need to wait and see. It's already been displayed to the full. What will she be five years from now? What difference can it possibly make?

You have to have seen her walk, have seen her get off the Metro with a broken heel in *En cas de malheur,* to realize that one day she must have had these very same experiences herself. She must have put on her first high-heel shoes—when she was sixteen—and gone out into the street and walked a hundred yards. It must have happened the first time she tried to turn. To transcend talent in this way, to deny the whole moral infrastruc-ture of the world, makes you look at yourself with a hard eye. That's the way it is with Queen Bardot. People accept that it isn't Princess Margaret's fault if she's the daughter of the king of En-gland. But they think that since Bardot isn't the daughter of the kind of England, there's no reason she should be as famous as Princess Margaret.

As everyone knows, for the past one thousand nine hundred fifty-eight years, a fundamental falsehood has lain at the heart of Christianity. Men and women no longer dare to look directly at sights that might provoke lust or envy. I've heard men say of Queen Bardot: "I wouldn't want her for all the gold in the world." Sure. There's no risk in saying such things. And wives are pleased to hear their husbands say them. Since Queen Bardot embodies a threat to the institution of marriage (what man wouldn't be tempted to do as Gabin did?), to look directly at her would be to commit an act, a reprehensible act, of terrifying courage. And anyway, they say she's not a nice person.

Whereas Ava Gardner and Rita Hayworth aroused temptations of tragic and mortal passion (the word *myth* being tiresome, I deliberately choose not to use it of them), Queen Bardot arouses temptations of adulterous love, of an unexpected windfall. She suggests that any man may meet his Queen Bardot. Her beauty is not fatal but amiable. She is beautiful like a woman but cuddly like a child. She has a simple, honest look. She plays primarily on the narcissistic love that a man feels for himself. If a woman like that were given to me, the man thinks, I would make her over in my own image. She would become dependent on me, and I could at last give free rein to my desire to have someone in my power. For a perfect woman always gives a man the substance on which he can exercise his omnipotence, to the point of barbarism. Queen Bardot stands just at the point where morality presumably ends and the jungle of amorous immorality begins: a territory from which Christian boredom is banished.

France-Observateur, 1958

Callas

The original French version of this article has been lost. This translation, by Adrian Foulke, appeared in *Vogue* in 1965.

Her name lacks by chance only one letter to form the anagram of the world's most famous opera house. Even the sound is close: La Scala.

She has reigned for sixteen years over the world's stages, peerless, incomparable; her presence assumes the proportions of an event, as she passes from capital to capital raising havoc, being rejected, worshiped, extolled to the skies, execrated. She is, in a word, indestructible. Like it or not, Callas is the inspired force that has revived the art of acting in opera, and in so doing has not only restored youth and life to opera but has borne it to the highest peak of its power.

With her, opera singing ceases to be mere vocal prowess. She quickens the poetry that lies hidden within song, she reawakens the magic of the tale. All the Sleeping Beauties have been awaiting her. For fifty years, what eye did Tosca cause to shed a tear—until Callas took her in hand?

She is a Gorgon, a Medusa. And very nineteenth century. She resembles our image of Sarah Bernhardt and Duse. She was formed, one would say, in the floral style of the turn of the century; surely she has known d'Annunzio, Puccini. That craggy face belongs to some period other than ours. The large features. The wide mouth, like the mouth of some deep-sea fish. An outsize mouth designed for the devouring of life. She is one who alters very little, who is beyond affectation, beyond coquetry, even. She is the most beautiful of the ugly women of her time. This magnificent ugliness belongs to her alone; it has never been fashionable, as with Marlene Dietrich or Brigitte Bardot. The secret of this face is that it must be seen at the distance which separates orchestra from stage. Behind the dazzling fires of footlights no one is so beautiful as this ugly woman: There she shines. Her body? It is motion, motion that supports the head, the dark, dramatic voice that has led thousands of listeners to a form of art that before her they were unable to love.

To indulge in the rages, the caprices, and even in other still more serious lapses in order to become what nature made you—does this make one an *arriviste?* I think not. What is done is done out of necessity, rather like sacrifice, in a battle that has ceased to be a single-handed private combat. When one is Callas, "personal" ambition becomes a duty toward the rest of us. Her secret, I believe, is that a message was given her before her time, and she understood that she would have the power needed to bring her art, all art, to its apogee. Without hypocrisy, with the energy of a lioness, she has battled in the name of this other woman who was contained within her, the woman with whom we now confuse her—Callas.

Vogue, 1965

Socquet Jeanne

The first time I saw Jeanne Socquet's painting was in 1973 at the Valérie Schmidt Gallery in rue Mazarine. On the walls were women, tall, wide, smooth, flowing, dripping with color. Some were dragging wheels. Others were in places invaded by wheels—wheels with teeth, from machines, and wheels without teeth. Lost way up at the top of the canvas were their heads, with heavy, drooping eyelids from beneath which emanated lifeless gazes, identical in all the figures. All bore the dead weight, the vast, open wound, of enormous, languid, bloody mouths—some had several mouths. All these women with wheels were *maneuvered* from outside, manipulated from someplace outside themselves. I recognized them all. And I smiled at them, overcome by a kind of joy. Yes, I was happy to see them again, as though I had entered their lair without knowing that I had expected to enter, as though I saw them at last without ever knowing that I had been expecting to see them. I noticed that I was smiling at them only after the smile formed on my lips. Joy had come to me without my knowledge, unpredictable and very intense, better informed than I, in advance of my conscious intelligence. For I did not realize right away who these women were, these wheel-women and gear-women who surrounded me, suspended, inserted into surfaces of very vivid color by means of soft, velvety curves mysteriously signaled on canvas by the curves of the mouths and wheels. Little by little these huge whores, these great, gawking prostitutes emerged from *my own history*. My sisters? Yes. Sisters, these uprooted Barbarellas, shorn of fiction, with their mute, vaginalike mouths? Yes. Sisters, these women of the now gutted boudoirs, like concentration camps of the still recent past, boudoirs in which they lay in the golden shadow of gentlemen who had made vast sums in iron and steel? Yes. Exhumed from the cemeteries of Montmartre beyond the crumbling bordellos, these ladies of the night were my sisters. So violent was the spectacle that I couldn't tear my eyes away. Having made the round of the gallery, I started over again, to have another look at my sisters with their wheels, at these women staring with sightless eyes, unearthed from the awfulness of woman's history. And I experienced pleasure because they had been discovered and magnificently resurrected so that I might see them at last outside the cultural apparatus of the male epic. Extracted from that epic for me, a woman.

This time, this year, Jeanne Socquet has captured for painting, in painting, another stratum of reality. A stratum contemporary with us, alive, on the move: the reality of the streets, the buses, the subways, the office buildings, the parks, the universities, and the "architectural complexes," the reality that pullulates around us and within us. This series of paintings is our series. The figures this time are both male and female—here sex has absolutely no meaning. I saw them, and the smile returned to my lips, even more intense this time but coupled with fear. I was happy and terrified. The paintings are of heads—your head, my head—heads cut off at the chin—a fabulous festival of our heads, which Jeanne Socquet has set against the frenzy and the rot of capitalist society. Heads of idiots and fools, of braggarts, of the self-satisfied, of the always happy, of people shot through with arrows but still always happy, of people suffering wounds but still as humble and content as ever, round heads, pear-shaped mugs, heads with dewlaps, expressionless fatheads, plump heads with no mouths, tiny heads with very large mouths, real balloon heads with hens' asses for mouths and, higher up, pigs' eyes gleaming with the self-satisfaction of the person who "never complains." The silent majority? Yeah. Suddenly immense, stretching as far as the eye can see, a vast expanse of the humiliated, the beaten, the crushed, and other oppressed victims, stuffed to the gills with the morality of fear by the reigning capitalist oligarchies. This, too, is great political painting, this painting by the woman Jeanne Socquet. The late denizens of the bordellos of Montmartre stare at these heads, the heads of our fools. There they are, in a corner of the canvas, looking at us. The heads are unaware of being looked at by those figures of another season, by the gaze of *history,* a gaze that is empty, merely present: a reminder—in code, as it were—of the age-old repression of Woman.

One leaves the show wondering what they might have done to us, what mortal injury—at which we smile in fear—and the thought is so overwhelming that the mind wanders, that it is tempted to look beyond oppression, beyond the political explanation. EVERYBODY IS RECOGNIZABLE. And the wonderful thing is that they're all our brothers: the fool and the braggart, the self and the other, the one who "never complains" and the victim of oppression. We've all emerged from the same horror. We've all been plucked from that horror by Jeanne Socquet. And she loves us all in the same way: with communist love.

I made her acquaintance a short time ago and asked her if I might write about her painting. I know her because of her painting, but is it really possible to know her in any other way? The identification is so powerful that I don't think so. This painting that she does is, in my opinion, very great painting. I have rarely seen such power at work or an investigation of such scope. Some would say that the pictorial function in her work operates in two ways. It describes, and then it moves on. It does not stop. Whatever is encountered is drawn in, accumulated, incorporated into the body of the painting itself, which here gives a very powerful sense of having existed before. And this insatiable body is constantly assimilating and devouring more, gaining strength, fortifying its muscles and its love. For here, around the muscle and sinew of painting, is a woman.

"Love underlies all of it. Without love I wouldn't have noticed these people."

She is speaking of the fools, the brutes, the whole population with whom she shares her existence. I ask:

"Does it all come from the madwomen you observed at Charenton?"

"Yes." She says it all comes from that. "The mouths too?" I ask.

"Yes. In lunatics the mouth is missing from the face. Their features are no longer tied together. Their faces have decomposed."

"Why are mouths so important in your painting?"

"To me the mouth is the most important feature. I don't know why it has such importance. Possibly because we use the mouth when we try to speak or when we eat or when we cry. Perhaps for all those reasons."

The fantastic sketches made at Charenton are *portraits* of insane women. None of them describes madness. Jeanne Socquet adopts a strictly individualistic approach. Similarly, the faces in this show are of individuals, seen one at a time, person by person. Socquet's painting has nothing to do with describing "the people on the Metro" or "the people at Charenton." And when she eventually shows the fantastic series of "people receiving blows," the individual will also be there, beneath the flattened or twisted face, behind the striking fist. Similarly, in the series of "Stars," a series of cold and terrifying vampires, the individual is also present, and so is the painter's love. And even in the series of "Dogs," which depicts the fat lap dogs of Parisian concierges and the treasured doggy-woggies of the French bourgeoisie, that same love is present, and so is the individuality of each dog, reduced by oppression, however indirect, to the same state of horror as its owner-mistress. In Jeanne Socquet's work, the more insignificant something is outside the canvas, the more it exists in the canvas: this woman is incapable of the theoretical error of believing that that which cannot be seen has less existence than that which can be seen.

What is there in this painting that has so captivated me and that plunged me, whenever I look at it, into what I can only call a state of organic reflection, a mood of readiness to receive, to dissolve myself, to confound myself without prejudice or hesitation or defensiveness with the act of Seeing? No doubt it is the novel nature of the painting, which with animal stealth calmly and irresistibly *penetrates* what lies outside it. Somewhere within herself Jeanne Socquet has knowledge of the essential thing. She has not stopped at the half-way point but has pressed on as far as it is possible to go, alone, without reference of any kind to the painting of men, which surveys the city with its watchtowers and cops. She has pressed on, without fanfare or anger but in a natural manner, toward a painting of her own. She brushes aside the stupid nostalgia that many women feel when confronted with male thinking, for she is aware that woman has her own ideas within herself and that in order to exist she has only to begin setting those ideas down in a language of her own. This peasant from the Nord, rugged and calm, is like an unspoiled primitive, a sort of primordial woman loosed by nature itself in the ancient city of man.

Notes to the 1974 show at
the Valérie Schmidt Gallery

At the Bottom of the Sea:
A Show of Paintings by Marie-Pierre Thiébaut

Where are we? At the bottom of the sea? Inside a woman? In a well? Inside a fruit? I think it's both the bottom of the sea and the bottom of the womb. The primordial, universal environment, the marine symbiosis.

The strength and grace of Marie-Pierre Thiébaut's sculptures come, I think, from that. The region in which she works is precisely the common, undifferentiated region of a life retrieved from the waters, from the salt. What interests her is the first instincts of living things, their attempts to escape from the primal magma. She searches for the roots of movement and, crucially, does not isolate or capture it. Rather, she observes and tries to "turn" with the motion, to join it. Which leads to this: You recognize her sculptures as being already deeply felt. Everything communicates with everything else, but ordinarily one does not see this. Here, suddenly, one does see it.

Inside a closed oyster, or, if you prefer, in a bed formed by two rocks placed side by side, we find plantlike breasts that have grown in the rocks' shadow. Under the hooked shell of a sea creature, a sea turtle, we see a swell. In one sculpture the womblike composition is also a forest, an open, moving forest through which children pass. In another a woman's sexual organ is also a flower, a starfish, a floral spray with corollas of coral. By contrast, the breast is enclosed in a shell, immersed in the night of the body.

Male and female sex organs achieve a kind of animal coexistence, suggestive, perhaps, of a zoo in some remote paradise. The phalluses emerge from what Thiébaut calls "landscapes" and rise in the female waves of earth. Their erection is not dramatic but happy. The earth, underneath, is still asleep.

The sea is everywhere. Salt and the sea linger in the living basin in which our children swim, in their fish stage, in our bellies. As the trees of the forest grow out of the water, seeking their identity as trees, so our muscles grow in order to propel our children into the world and give them separate identities—in both cases, the same deliverance from the waters.

All of Marie-Pierre Thiébaut's sculptures could be enlarged to architectural dimensions. Even the smallest are by nature monumental. Why? Because their subject is not limited in space or time. It is the very essence of the nonsubject. A woman's sex that one can hold in the palm of the hand might well be erected as a monument in some city's main square.

Sorcières, 1972

"The Shades of Night," by Aki Kuroda

There are fourteen paintings in Aki Kuroda's exhibition. On the surface they are all similar. This superficial resemblance marks this group of paintings as having been done over the past three years. In reality the paintings are not alike. Aki Kuroda, I saw, was not painting the dark of night. He was painting this particular night, or that night, or some other night: night in general does not exist. Kuroda has called his fourteen canvases "The Shades of Night." The show is summed up by that plural.

Aki Kuroda starts out as though he were painting. He is in fact painting. He covers the entire canvas with white paint. He paints its entire *surface white*. Then he must wait until the paint dries. For days, perhaps weeks: I'm not sure. Then Aki Kuroda starts over. He acts as though he were painting. He paints. He covers the white canvas with black paint. Tracing the evolution of Kuroda's work, I see the thickness of time that he must amass on the *surface of the canvas* before he can approach that disfiguration of blackness that through the ages has been called "the painting." Everybody, I think, should see it as I do. *With black, then, he covers the white.* Now, even at this stage, in my view, the fear begins, because the black will remain forever on top of the white. And because for certain canvases, especially the most recent, it is no longer possible to say that the *black surface* is merely a covering of the white surface.

Something else happens. Yes, already, something else can be seen: irregularities, movements, barely visible accidents that happen, stand out, and then repeat themselves regularly. Perhaps you remember those *naked footprints* of a prehistoric man buried in clay thirty thousand years deep, the footsteps of *someone* who was passing by, who slipped and picked himself up and then, leaving the muddy path that preserved his footprints, vanished *forever.* In the end, the accumulation of accidents in the black layers produces a direction. The canvas takes on a direction. A direction it will keep forever. That is admirable. Yes, the tremors in the painting hand, in this case I think the right hand, give a general direction to the canvas, an orientation exactly like the orientation imposed by the *wind.* Whatever will cover the canvas when the journey is complete will be affected by this *wind.* Since the beginning of the world the *wind* has never passed in just this way over the sand or over anything else—never. It was never before the same *wind,* the same sand—never. Here, today, what passes before our eyes is the hand of Aki Kuroda. It is the *wind* striking the fresh and still liquid blackness, the wind that wrinkles the blackness as it would wrinkle the sand beneath it, or the surface of the sea.

After the black painting, more time is required. Time for what? Time enough for the black to dry, and perhaps a bit more. More *days, possibly weeks:* I'm not sure. At this point the ritual involves a sacrificial rite. There are additional phases invented by the painter, desired by him as trials of patience, deliberate delays, insisted upon and observed. The final touch takes just a few minutes. *With a calligrapher's brush* Aki Kuroda paints the final canvas in just a few minutes. On top of three weeks of black and white he works feverishly with a calligrapher's brush, and in a few minutes, with a single stroke, he will destroy the disposition of the black once and for all: *he will sign the painting.*

But I've forgotten something: sometimes, between the black and the destruction of the surface there is an intermediate stage, involving the drawing of a regular grid on the black, dividing it into equal parts—the lines of a notebook, or rain that falls straight from the top to the bottom of the canvas. This, I think, is an additional paroxysm of the sacrificial stage, adding still more unbelief, still more intoxication, still more time to the thickness of the canvas, still more ceremonial—but not the ceremonial of any cult, no indeed: all of this to reach the final minute, in which the whole fortune of time and life accumulated in the canvas is wagered. As patient as Aki Kuroda was, as slowly as he worked, so now he races like lightning and thunder: the greatest danger he faces is himself. This, above all, is Kuroda: this contest. Aki Kuroda lays out the field of massacre as carefully as the field of good fortune. We are with him. During this minute of painting Aki Kuroda evidently writes the *decisive sentence* that will allow him to leave the painting to others. But then, no, he starts over, writing *illegible* sentences, letting us see their illegibility *cloaked in paint*. Kuroda is thus *silent* about knowledge of the painting itself. He says that there is something to understand but you never know what, that there is something to be said but you never know how. The effort that I am making right now I see as conditioned by the silence established by Kuroda.

Kuroda is one step ahead of the silence. He does not illuminate what cannot be illuminated, what will not accept and cannot hold light: among millions of propositions, for example, that of thought, that of light, that of *painting*.

Notes to the 1980 show at the Maeght Gallery

Carlos d'Alessio

To tell the truth, I'm not really sure where Carlos Alessio comes from. They say Argentina, but the first time I heard his music I realized that he came from everywhere: I saw boundaries removed, defenses banished, and rivers flowing freely—rivers of music, and of desire. And I saw that I was as much a part of this Argentine nation, of this Vietnam of the South Pacific, as he, Carlos Alessio. What joy! I was very happy, and I asked him to do the music for a film of mine. He said yes. I said for free. And he said yes. And I left room in the images and dialogue for his music, and I explained to him that the film took place in a country that neither of us knew, colonial India—the vast twilight of leprosy and the hunger of Calcutta's lovers—and that both of us would have to invent it out of whole cloth. Which we did. And the film was made, he and I made it together. It was called *India Song*, and it was finished and taken from our hands, it left us, and now it is making its way through the world with the pain wrested from our

CARLOS D'ALESSIO

bodies, leaving us alone for it will never again be ours, just as we shall never again be together making the film. So there we are, left alone to make other music, other films, other songs, and to love each other so much, ever so much, if you only knew.

Album liner notes

"Rauque la ville," by Jean-Pierre Ceton

I've just finished reading Jean-Pierre Ceton's manuscript. Isavert is gone forever, the first to leave. I hear Vickie's stiff step leaving the railroad station after her departure. The book is finished for good. I am in the middle of my bedroom, as if paralyzed. It is three in the morning. I try to think of someone I can telephone to say, I want to tell you about a major event that nobody else knows about: a book has just been written. I stand in my room next to the closed book and telephone no one: I cannot. The book is there, the book that traveled through time; it is there like any other book, closed like any other book, with me, in my bedroom. It is alone. Without any relationship with anything other than itself, hence in relation with everything. I decide not to call anyone, not even Jean-Pierre Ceton, whom I hardly know. I'm afraid I won't know how to talk to him, afraid that I'll embarrass him. I decide to bear alone the stifling weight of this novella, this truth: yes, this truth, this book next to me into which I have been trans-

ported body and soul, with as piercing a pain as if I had written it
myself.

That is the clearest thing I can say. I do not know how to judge
this book; I cannot judge it. I do not see it. To perform on it the
usual critical surgery is something I cannot do. As after reading
any great work I might say: I do not know how it is written. In the
writing there may be admirable negligence as well as astonishing
knowledge. Both may be there. Both are there. The book has no
meaning. It proposes every possible meaning at once, but only
within its own meaning. Through its meaning it touches on every
other meaning, *without knowing that it does so*. It is alone. Yes, it
is alone in the midst of the world. It has swept away all fashion,
all models. It is alone, unaware of its power, innocent, free, innocent, but so remote, so truly remote, that this is not apparent, or
is barely apparent, can barely be felt—like the air. It will therefore be reviled and adored, adored and burned. Yes.

Yes, the word comes to me. A word comes to me: an immensity.
The truth is there. An immensity is contained within, shut up
within. You don't notice at first, you have to read on a ways, and
then, suddenly, there it is. It's like approaching a forest. The
ocean? a forest? an ocean? What is this? Where are we? In one of
those new plantations of human beings, one of those infinite cities restored to nature? Yes, that's it, swallowed up again. We're in
the midst of a new kind of nature, in a place yielded up to nature,
a vast city inhabited by transparent forms, by creatures that cannot be grasped and that cast no shadow, surrounded by a maze of
walls, hiding places, communicating enclosures, places to sleep
piled one on top of the other, whirlpools, precipices, dark places,
light places, hiding places, places to escape from *them*, to meet
one another, to recognize one another, places to do nothing, to
love one another, to kill one another, to love, meet, kiss, caress,
to love, to grow, to laugh, laugh, to love, to be alone on the brink
of death and then to find Maniaë and Leyo and to laugh with happiness and desire, to love, to grow, always, always, in every
sense, in one's own sense and in the sense of others. Not a word,
never, of moral poison. Yes, here there is an immensity. One
knows this, one sees it. Suddenly, as you're reading, you cross a
threshold and the book has no more bottom to it, no more walls,

it is outside you, it surrounds you, it swallows you up. Suddenly you stop reading as you had been reading: "Reading" is no longer the appropriate word. You've entered the city, I suppose. You walk. You go in. You want to keep Leyo from dying. You cry, you love, you walk, you go in.

Editions de Minuit, 1980

Conversation with Francis Bacon

"I don't draw. I begin by making all sorts of blots. I wait for what I call 'the accident': the blot with which the painting can begin. The blot is an accident. But if you rely on the accident, if you think you understand the accident, you're still going to do illustration, for the blot always looks like something.

"You can't understand the accident. If you could understand it, you'd also understand the way you're going to act. But the way you're going to act is unpredictable, you can never understand it. It's basically the technical imagination. I've thought a lot about what to call the unpredictable way you're going to act. 'Technical imagination' is all I've been able to come up with.

"The subject, mind you, is always the same. It's the change in the technical imagination that can turn the subject back on one's own nervous system.

"To imagine extraordinary scenes is not interesting from the point of view of painting. It's not imagination. True imagination is constructed by the technical imagination. The rest is imaginary imagination, which leads nowhere.

"That's why I can't read Sade. His work doesn't completely disgust me, but it bores me. And there are internationally known writers I can't read either. They write sensational stories, nothing more. But they don't have the technical sense.

"The true openings are always discovered by technicians. The technical imagination is instinct ungoverned by rules, which works to turn the subject back on the nervous system with the force of nature.

"There are young painters who dig a hole in the ground, take some dirt, and then show that dirt in an art gallery. That's silly, and it proves that they lack technical imagination. It's interesting that they want to change the subject so badly that they go so far as to take a lump of dirt and put it on a pedestal. But what's needed is that the 'force' that goes into digging up the dirt should be 'turned around.' Dig up the dirt, fine, but let them take it from their own personal system and make it with their technical imagination."

"Is the notion of progress in painting a false notion?"

"Yes. Take the paleolithic painting of northern Spain—I've forgotten the name of the cave. In those figures you see movements that have never been captured better. Futurism in its entirety is there. It's perfect stenography of movement."

"Is the notion of personal progress also false?"

"Less so. You work on yourself in order to force yourself to strip things ever more naked."

"What's the danger?"

"Systematization. And belief in the importance of the subject. The subject has no importance.

"Talent can regress, start over. The historical exceptions are Michelangelo, Titian, Velasquez, Goya, and Rembrandt. They never regressed."

"How does one progress?"

"Work. Work makes work. Do you agree?"

"No. You have to start somewhere. Without a starting point there's no point working. When I read certain books, I find that to write in a certain way is to write less than if one didn't write at all. That to read in a certain way is to read less than if one didn't read at all. And so on."

"It's the same with painting. But with the technical imagination you never know. It can go to sleep and then one day reawaken. The main thing is that it be there."

"Let's get back to the blots of color."

"Yes. I'm always hoping for a blot upon which I can build the 'apparition.'"

"The blots always come first?"

"Almost always. They're 'things that happen to me,' that happen through me, through my nervous system, which was created at the moment of my conception."

"Is the idea of the 'joy of painting' as silly as the idea of the 'joy of writing'?"

"Just as silly."

"Do you feel yourself in danger of dying when you're painting?"

"I become very nervous. You know Ingres cried for hours before he began to paint. Especially with portraits."

"Goya is supernatural."

"Perhaps not. But he's fabulous. He married forms with the air. His paintings seem to have been made with the stuff of the atmosphere. That's extraordinary, fabulous. The greatest Goya, in my opinion, is at Castres: *The Philippine Junta.*"

"How does painting stand today in the world?"

"In a bad pass. Because the subject was so difficult, people set off into abstraction. Logically, that seemed to be the right way for painting to proceed. But since one can do anything at all in abstract art, one ends up doing mere decoration. At that point it seems that the subject again becomes necessary, because only the subject brings all the instincts into play and forces you to look for and find the right means to express it. That brings us back, you see, to technique."

"You never painted before you were thirty?"

"No. Before that I was a drifter. How do you say that in French?"

"*Dérivant.*"

"I always looked at painting. And at some point I said, Why not me? I spent fifteen years trying to get somewhere. I started getting somewhere when I was forty-five. My good fortune was that I never learned painting from teachers."

"What about criticism of your work?"

"The critics have always been against me. All of them, always. Recently there have been a few who say I'm a genius and things like that, but it doesn't mean anything. I will be dead before I know who I am, because such knowledge takes time. Only with time can you begin to see value."

"We've often spoken about the 'accident.'"

"I can't define it. I can only talk around it. In his letters Van Gogh, too, talks around painting. His 'brushstrokes,' at the end of his life—there's no explanation for the force of his brushstrokes."

"Try, from outside."

"All right: If you take some stuff and throw it against a wall or a canvas, you immediately find the features of a person that you're trying to capture. No deliberate action is involved. You get an immediate sketch of the character that has nothing to do with illustrating a subject. When house painters paint patches on a wall before starting a job, they're doing the same thing, making an immediate preliminary sketch. The American abstract expressionists tried to paint the same way, but with the strength of the material.

"It's not enough. It's still decoration.

"The strength is not and should not be in the force with which the material is thrown. The strength must be entirely congealed in the subject. The material that is thrown against the wall—that could be the accident, you see. What comes next is the technical imagination."

"Duchamp?"

"He ruined American painting for a hundred years. Everything derives from him, and everyone. What is peculiar, very peculiar indeed, is that his painting was the most aesthetic of the twentieth century. But his touch was so sure, and his intelligence."

"Is the accident the same thing as luck or chance?"

"Yes. All those words are the same."

"What is the special moment? How is it defined?"

"It's when the 'muscles' are working well. Then the blots seem to have more meaning, more strength."

"Everything is concrete."

"Everything. I don't understand my paintings any better than anyone else. I see them as outlets for various levels of my technical imagination. No one understands what is new about painting. There's no one to whom you can show a painting who is likely to see what is new in it."

"You say that you don't understand, yet your paintings sparkle with intelligence."

"Is that possible?"

"I think so. I knew a little girl who asked, 'What is heat when there is no one who feels hot?' I ask you: What is intelligence when thought is absent? What is intelligence when no one experiences or uses it for critical ends, for purposes of judgment, and so on? Are we not very close to what you call instinct?"

"Yes, I agree. In my portraits and other paintings I want to experience the same shock that you feel in life when you look at 'nature.'"

"And for that you think you have to work as though you were an imbecile?"

"Absolutely, yes. Sometimes the critical sense revives and for a moment the painting becomes visible. Then it disappears again."

"When do you work?"

"In the morning, with the light. In the afternoon I go to bars or gambling halls. Sometimes I see friends. In order to work I must be absolutely alone. No one else can be in the house. My instinct cannot work with other people present—and it's worse when they're people you love. It can work only in freedom."

La Quinzaine littéraire, 1971

A Brilliant Work:
L'Opoponax, by Monique Wittig

Yesterday I read the first article to appear on Monique Wittig's book, *L'Opoponax* [translated into English by Helen Weaver, *The Opoponax* (London, 1966)]. What I feared has come to pass: the author of the article read a different Opoponax from the one I read.

My Opoponax is possibly, indeed almost certainly, the first modern book to be written about childhood. My Opoponax does away with ninety percent of the books that have been written about childhood. It marks the end of a certain kind of literature, for which I thank heaven. The book is not only admirable, it is also important, for it is governed by an iron rule that is never, or almost never, broken. That rule is to use nothing but purely descriptive material and purely objective language. The latter assumes its full meaning here. It is the very language that children use to order and elaborate their world, but here transformed by the author into plainsong. What this comes down to is that my

Opoponax is a literary masterpiece, because it is written in the very language that Opoponax would use.

Do not be frightened: adults may not know that they speak Opoponax, but they do. They have only to read Monique Wittig's book to remember. Unless their eyes are very tired from reading a woefully false literature—that can happen, even to those who make their careers in the literary business.

A Fortress

What is this book about? Children. Ten or a hundred little boys and girls who are known by the names they've been given but who can also exchange those names for new ones. It's about a thousand little girls who sweep down on you like a tidal wave, which is indeed what the book is about: a vast, fluid element, like the sea. A crop, a tide of children carried along by a single wave: for when the book begins they are very, very young, in the depths of an endless childhood. Véronique Legrand is about three, I'd say.

At first the great wave rolls, it moves forward, it teems with the thousand smaller waves of which it is composed. These coexist, one following another with the rhythm of a fusillade and, I would say, in strict order. And then each of the little waves spreads out, slows down, rides over other waves and absorbs them until all are mixed together: childhood is aging. With extraordinary art the author contrives to make us feel this aging without our being aware of it. As with our own children we wonder what is happening, we are astonished. The age of multiplication comes, and then the age of Latin. But beware: if childhood is growing old, it is still childhood, still lodged within that impregnable fortress with its impenetrable walls. For the first time we understand that we cannot enter. We are invited to look and to see. Childhood takes place, it takes shape, it breathes before our very eyes.

The pace is just right. Time flows as from a deep well and fills us as it fills the childhood we are watching.

In the beginning there is a little girl who peels an orange, who makes a mouthful of the whole sky, of another little girl who is dead, and of everything, everything. And then the little girl moves on to another orange. She devours another orange. As

quick as lightning she combs another sky with her eyes. She
endures an hour of writing "sentences" in her notebook. And
then—then something happens. Between devouring, say, the
first orange and the second sky a secret tremor sets in. Between
making the gingerbread man and dissecting the butterfly something happens, but the little girl who made the ginger man and
the little girl who unmade the butterfly are the same.

At the end of childhood, when the book is closed and the walls
of the fortress crack, the link is made forever. The mind is already
poisoned by tremors of the heart. No longer do they play together, sharing their lives. Friendship is born.

Ideal guardians of the walls, all alike, anonymous like the substance of adulthood itself, the nuns of catholicity pass one by one
through the corridors and dormitories. Against their dull, black
skirts beat the currents of childhood. In the shadow of their devotion the terrible, virginal, pagan scrutiny of life and death
takes place.

A bishop dies. What ensues upon this death? In the pomp and
gold of the episcopal funeral, in the shadow of the nave, in the
shadow of all things made to be seen, beneath all things, a little
girl's hair is noticed by her neighbor, another little girl. How
beautiful it is. A discovery, the way the hair of the kneeling girl
moves in space: her hair moves as she does—she moves it—but
according to its own law. The hair breathes next to the little girl,
but upon her head, like a plant upon the earth. Not one adjective
is used in describing this discovery, which is the discovery of
beauty. The movement of the hair is described in the same way as
the blaring of the organs that accompanies the mass for the dead.
The music causes the walls to crumble. It is everywhere, while in
the meantime, below, surrounded by it on all sides, a child's hair
emerges from the primordial darkness and is seen by another
child. And the nuns pass by, blind witnesses to a beatitude as dazzling as their own, but different.

We Have All Written This Book

The nuns are useful. In this book one sees just how useful. By
marking the time of childhood with nonsensical and unstated ob-
ligations, they offer children the freedom to transgress.

There are also, if I remember correctly, unforgettable wars that take place in the age of Latin. Little girls are whipped with nettles, thighs are lacerated, traitors are found out. One child waits for other children to steal a large iron bar, for no particular purpose. The other children do not show up. At that moment, perhaps, dawn resembles a little what we call dawn. But ever so little.

I shall end here. We have all written this book: you and I. But only one of us has discovered this Opoponax that all of us have written, whether we like it or not. The separation takes place once the book has been closed. My Opoponax, my own, is a masterpiece.

France-Observateur, 1964

Leek Soup

People think they know how to make it. It seems so easy. Too
often they're not careful. It should cook anywhere from fifteen
to twenty minutes, not two hours. All French women overcook
vegetables and soups. It's better to put the leeks on while the
potatoes are boiling; the soup will stay green and have a much
better fragrance. And you've got to use the right amount of leeks:
two average-sized leeks will do nicely for just over two pounds of
potatoes. In restaurants this soup is never good: it's always over-
cooked (or reheated) or, as cooks say, too "long." It's sad and
dreary, just another of those "vegetable soups" that no provincial
restaurant in France can do without. You have to make it deliberately and carefully and not "forget it on the fire," which will
quickly destroy its characteristic flavor. You can serve it either
straight or with butter or *crème fraîche*. You can also add crou-
tons when the soup is served. If you do, you should call it by
a different name. Make one up. That way the children will eat
it more readily than if you simply call it leek and potato soup.
It takes time, years, to discover the flavor of this soup, which

children are forced to eat on a variety of pretexts (soup makes you grow, soup sweetens the personality, and so on). Nothing in French cooking can match the simplicity or necessity of leek soup. It could only have been invented in a western region on a winter's night by a still young woman of the local bourgeoisie, who on that particular night simply couldn't face the thought of another heavy sauce—and possibly of many other things as well, if only she knew. This soup the body happily laps up. There's no ambiguity here: this is not *garbure* [a soup made of cabbage, bacon, and conserve of goose—Trans.], not a soup to nourish you or warm you up. It's just a refreshing soup without meat. The body laps it up in great gulps, cleanses itself, purifies itself, tastes the first green of the season. The muscles' thirst is slaked. Its odor spreads quickly through the house, a common smell, like the smell of the food of the poor or the labor of women or sleeping animals or the vomit of newborns. You can want to do nothing and then decide instead to do this: make leek soup, I mean. Between the will to do something and the will to do nothing is a thin, unchanging line: suicide.

Sorcières, 1976

Thin, Yellow Children

. . . It was during her siesta that we stole mangoes. Mangoes—certain mangoes, not yet ripe—were deadly, she said. In the flat, plump core there sometimes lurked a black animal that one could swallow, and that, once swallowed, migrated to the stomach and gnawed it from the inside. Mother said these frightening things, and we believed her. Father was dead, we were poor, and she had three children she was trying to "raise." She was the queen, unchallenged, purveyor of food and love. But when it came to mangoes she seemed less strong. We disobeyed her and when she found us dripping with sticky juice after her siesta, she beat us. But we did it again. We always did it again. The eldest of the three children was in Europe. We two younger ones she kept with her. We were small and thin, my brother and I, little half-breeds, more yellow than white. Inseparable. She beat us together: dirty little Annamites, she said. She, she was French, she wasn't born out there. I must have been eight. I watched her at night, in her bedroom, in her nightgown. She walked around the

234

house and I looked at her wrists, her ankles. I didn't say anything. That they were too thick. That they were different. I thought she was different. Heavier, more voluminous. And that pink-colored flesh.

My only relative: my agile little brother, so thin, with slit eyes, crazy, silent, who at six climbed the giant mango trees and at fourteen killed black panthers along the rivers of the Elephant Range. What love, child. What love for your dead little brother. But she, she wasn't crazy about mangoes. And while she slept, in the magical quiet of her siestas, we thin little monkeys filled our bellies, bellies of a different race from hers. And so we became Annamites, you and I. She gave up hope of making us eat bread. We liked only rice. We spoke a foreign language. We went barefoot. She was too old. She couldn't get into a foreign language. We didn't even try to teach her. She wore shoes. And once she suffered a sunstroke because she hadn't worn a hat, and she screamed, she shouted that she wanted to go back to the northern hemisphere, to wheat and raw milk and cold weather, to her family of farmers, to Frévent in Pas-de-Calais, which she had left behind. And we, you and I, in the shadows of that colonial dining room, we watched her screaming and crying, with that abundant pink and red body, that rubicund good health. How could she be our mother? How is it possible? Our mother—when we were so thin, our skin was so yellow, and the sun didn't bother us? We Jews. I remember, the sunstroke happened at Phnom Penh. I looked at this woman, twice strange, twice a stranger. The memory is precise, probably crucial: yes, but the question has become a part of me, it flows in my veins. Eventually it would become external. Later, when we were fifteen, we asked ourselves: Are we really our father's children? Look. Look—we're half-breeds. We never had an answer. No problem: we knew that mother had been faithful, that the source of the miscegenation lay elsewhere. That elsewhere is endless. Our ineffable belonging to the land of mangoes, to the black water of the south, to the rice paddies is a mere detail. We know that. We confined ourselves to the mute depths of childhood, depths in our case magnified by the astonishment of people who saw us.

When we were bigger, people said: Think carefully. Did your

mother ever tell you where your father was when she was expecting you? Hadn't he gone to Plombières in France for treatment? We never gave it a thought: we knew that mother had been faithful to father and that the truth was something else, something we couldn't tell them about. I still know it: I don't know a thing. People said to us: Wasn't it the food and the sun? The food turns the skin yellow, and the sun narrows the eyes to slits, no? No. The scientists are categorical: such things do not happen, according to those who know. We don't ask any questions. As when we were six we didn't look at each other. We were a single foreign body, welded together by rice and stolen mangoes and mudfish and other cholera-infested filth that she didn't allow us to eat. The only thing clear and incontrovertible is this: we weren't the children she wanted. One day she said to us: I've bought some apples, fruit from France. You're French, you must eat apples. We tried and spit them out. She screamed. We said we were choking, that they tasted like cotton, that they had no juice, that it was impossible to swallow. She gave up. Meat, too, we spit out. We liked only freshwater fish cooked in brine of *nuoc-mam*. We liked only rice, the sublimely insipid flavor of rice from the boats that smelled like their cotton cargoes and the thin soups sold by the itinerant merchants of the Mekong. When we took the ferry at night, mother bought us duck soup. On the sampans charcoal fires burned under earthenware pots. The whole river smelled of wood fires and boiled herbs. Mother, worried, reminded us that in Vinh Long the week before, a whole street at the post had come down with cholera. The street was quarantined, and the hospitals were full. We went on eating, deaf, weaned.

Sorcières, 1976

The Horror of Such Love

Someone said, "Your child is dead." It was an hour after the delivery. The mother superior went to open the curtains and the May sunlight streamed into the room. I had noticed the child when the nurse carried it out. I hadn't seen it. The next day I asked, "What was he like?" They told me, "He's blond with a tinge of red. He has high brows like you. He looks like you."

"Is he still there?"

"Yes. Until tomorrow."

"Is he cold?"

R—— answered, "I haven't touched him, but he probably is. He's very pale." He hesitated, then said, "He is beautiful. That's because of death, too, I think."

I asked to see him. R—— said no. I asked the mother superior. She said no, that it wasn't worth the trouble. They had told me where he was, on the left side of the labor room. I couldn't move. I was worn out. I'd labored on my back. I didn't move. "What is his mouth like?"

"He has your mouth," R—— said.

Every hour: "Is he still there?"

People said, "I don't know."

I couldn't read. I looked out the open window, looked at the leaves on the locust trees growing along the embankment of the railway line that skirted the clinic. It was very hot. One night Sister Margaret was on duty. I asked her, "What are the going to do with him?"

She said, "I'd like nothing better than to stay with you. But you must go to sleep. Everyone is asleep."

"You're nicer than the mother superior. You'll go and get my baby for me, won't you? You'll leave him here for just a moment, won't you?"

"You can't be serious!" she shouted.

"Yes, I am serious. I'd like to have him here for an hour. He's mine."

"It's impossible. He's dead. I can't give you your dead baby."

"I'd like to see him and touch him. Just ten minutes."

"It's out of the question. I won't do it."

"Why not?"

"It will make you cry. You'll be sick. It's better not to see them in these cases. I'm used to it."

The next day, finally, in order to keep me quiet they told me that they burned the bodies. It all happened between May 15 and May 31 in 1942. I told R——, "I don't want any more visitors, except for you." Stretched out on my back, facing the locusts. The skin of my stomach stuck to my back, I was so empty. The child was no longer there. We were no longer together. He had died a separate death. An hour ago, a day ago, a week ago. A separate death, the end of a life that we had lived together for nine months but that he had left on his own. My belly had collapsed: a limp cloth, a rag, a burial shroud, nothing, a door, emptiness. Yet it had carried that child; within its slimy, velvety heat that marine fruit had grown. The light had killed it. It had been bludgeoned to death by its solitude in space. People said, "It's not so bad when they die in childbirth. It's better that way." Was it so bad? I think so. Precisely that: the coincidence between his coming into the world and his death. Nothing. I had nothing left. The emptiness was terrible. I had not had a child, not even for an hour. I was forced to imagine everything. Immobile, I imagined.

The child who is here now, who is asleep, laughed a while ago. He laughed at a giraffe that someone gave him. He laughed and it sounded like laughter. There was a breeze, and a little bit of that laugh reached my ears. So I raised the hood of his carriage a little and gave him back his giraffe so he would laugh again, and I put my head inside the hood so that I could take in all the sound of that laugh. Of my child's laugh. I put my ear against the shell and heard the sound of the sea. The thought that this laugh might vanish in the wind was unbearable to me. I caught it. My child: I had him. Sometimes when he yawns, I breathe in his yawn, the air from his yawn. "If he dies, I will have had this laugh." I know that he can die. I appreciate the full horror of such love.

Sorcières, 1976

Crime: The Pleasant Dream

I remember a dream that I dreamed often during the war. It was a pleasant dream. I dreamed of exterminating Germany. All the German leaders and all the German people would be brought together and killed, and the German earth they had trodden would be covered over in its entirety by a tombstone, which would render it forever unusable and unsuitable to serve as the fatherland of any nation whatsoever. I was punishing the German people and the German land for having killed the Jews. This dream was quite violent, terrifying, and intoxicating. I recognize it even today as a creative dream. I was creating the destruction of the Nazi Eden—for it was indeed the destruction of a Garden of Eden. *I was making* the desert. In short, I was behaving as God might have done. I was indiscriminately punishing the innocent and the guilty, the land as well as its inhabitants, the trees as well as the people. In a sense I was shaping destiny.

Everybody has had dreams like this. Everybody still has them. What differentiates one person from another is that some people, when they wake up, will admit it and others will not. I report my dreams. I believe I always have. I will say now that I am dreaming of the murder of every Soviet leader, without exception. And I'm also dreaming of the total extermination of the Soviet armies occupying Prague and Kabul. I unleash the monsters that dwell within me and answer murder with murder. I kill happily. I am powerless to oppose my dream, as you are powerless to oppose yours. Murder is calming, it puts me at ease, it lets me sleep. The difference between the Nazis, the Stalinists, and myself is that *they* don't know what criminals they are, whereas *I* do. The difference is not between those who dream and those who do not, but between those who see and those who don't see that the entire world is contained in every individual, and that every individual is a potential criminal. The Nazis were naive. They behaved naively, as though they held the right to discriminate between life and death. Where I dream, they acted. The Germans became professional criminals because they didn't recognize their crimes as a déjà vu of world history, a known datum of the history of humanity. Out of the naiveté of their dreams they created the criterion of a *natural crime*. They dreamed up an intruder whose mere existence supposedly prevented the flourishing of the Aryans: for that they invented a race. It's frightening to remember such fantasies, for which there appears to be no remedy. To forget that at any time any nation may witness the rise of a Hitler, a Stalin, a Pinochet, or a Shah of Iran, or his successors is to take the first step toward crime. To join in the game of power, whether its origins lie in the Marxist dungheap or in injustice, poverty, revenge, or religion, is to forget that one is a citizen of the world; it is to take sides against the human race. This is indeed the first step toward crime. To fail to see the other is to fail to see one's own shadow: the substantial nature that we all share. In my dream I kill Nazis and Stalinists for one simple reason: they do not see that they are inevitably, *fatally*, citizens of the world. Nationalism is already a crime. The German forest was Aryan, and so were German dogs. The German good was Aryan. This was foolishness, of course, but we see the same foolishness in any *localized* attempt to take possession of nature or art. The French insistence on the "French cultural heritage" is no less foolish. The worst thing that can happen is for there to be people who do not see or even sense—however dimly, apart from education of any kind—that every person is inevitably connected with every other: such people are deprived of the sense of eternity. After the war the Germans had forgotten how to play the music of Stravinsky. They had no idea how much their crime had set them apart from other men. It took them years to learn once more how to play and conduct *Jewish* music. The infantile quality of Soviet art exhibits similar backwardness. Here despair assumes such proportions that one is tempted to believe that it is the greatest of all our despairs. I mean the despair of those who see, who are part of, the whole, as opposed to the others, who distinguish themselves from the whole but in the manner of animals, based on knowledge of their strength rather than of the weakness of their victims, their prey—mirror images of themselves. This irreducible and final difference is *natural*. It obliges us to dismiss as utopian any belief in the perfectibility of man. One can modify behavior or replace a severed leg with a wooden prosthesis, but one cannot substitute a manufactured sensibility for a sensibility that does not exist. Nothing sticks in this void, nothing can take hold. And the void is natural because it is severed from the whole or, one might say, from the intelligence. I know of a young psychotic whose parents educated him word by word, gesture by gesture, for years in order to prepare him to cope with almost any situation he might be expected to face, given his circumstances. This education was successful. It worked. The young man had answers for nearly every question, even those questions not anticipated by his teachers; he had a plausible, universal answer. The weather is nice. How is your wife? It rained yesterday. Yes, summer is late this year. I don't quite understand what you're saying. It worked so well that you almost couldn't tell. Except for one thing: *the young man could not dance in step.* A hundred dancing lessons made no difference. He simply *did not hear* the beat and, had he heard it, wouldn't have understood the required connection with the movement of his body. This shortcoming was so obvious, so terrible to behold, that it revealed his illness to all who saw him. It is obvious that the American woman who goes around today in a sealskin coat, when the whole world is flooded with pictures of the massacre of seals, is so gravely ill that nothing can be done to cure her. She can't hear the music either. She doesn't know a thing about it. She's outside it. And her *innocent wearing* of the snowy fur is the clue to all the other consequences of her failure to exist. She must not dream. She must be so close to the crime that she's unaware of it. Although such people are among us, we do not know them. When suddenly we find out who they are, it's like waking up one morning next to an officer of the S.S. There was once a tree in the courtyard of a building. It had been there for perhaps a hundred years. When the owners of the building met, the question of whether or not to keep the tree was raised. Of the twenty-five owners, one wanted the tree cut down. People looked fearfully at one another. The vote had been secret. No one ever knew who voted to have the tree cut down. What I am trying to say is that nature is you as well as I or the American woman who wears the sealskin or the tenant who voted to cut down the tree or the twenty-year-olds who killed Pierre Goldman, who break off the branches of young trees, and who kill dogs, frogs, and elderly suburbanites. To say that such actions are due to frustrations experienced in childhood—is this to speak the truth? I don't think so, and I've never really thought so, not even when I thought I did. The frustration is always there, in each and every one of us, as inevitable as its cause. The child wants everything, but not even his mother can give it to him. Frustration is as inevitable as teething and weaning. I believe in ontological differences between people, in evil, in the curse. Yes, I believe in that; there are plenty of sophisms in nature. Recently, a fellow from the north of France told me that the count of Paris had put up for sale the forests he owned in Thiérarche, huge, beautiful forests comprising a hundred or more acres. The buyers of these forests, he said—he who bought a small piece for himself—were two ministers in the current French government. I refused to believe that anyone would want to own for himself alone a forest the size of a country, that anyone would fight for such a thing or have the time to fight for it when presumably he had devoted his life to the welfare of the French people. Then I heard the story again. And now I've repeated it to you. Some time before that I saw an unforgettable note in the newspaper *Le Monde*. It was reported that after the French government expropriated a large plot of land at Larzac [where it wished to build a military base—Trans.], suspicious peasants had put their land up for sale, and these properties had been bought up by legislators, including some who had voted for the original expropriation; their intention, we are told, was to resell the land to the government later on. Thiérarche and Larzac—it's like waking up next to an S.S. officer. Maybe all these people are the precursors of the final era. The leaders of the last procession, the forerunners of death. And then there are those who steal the rations of the victims of famine in the Sahel. Or those who steal the food of dying Cambodians, who would trade a truckload of rice—the survival of a people—for a hundred grams of private gold: I mean the glorious people's army of so-called Communist Vietnam. Yes. Maybe these are the first people to cross the threshold of the end of the world. Somebody has to be first. What comes from nature and from man is so contradictory, so absurd, and so peculiar that one has to wonder if these aren't the first signs of the final destruction of life. In that case these people would be, in all innocence, the first agents of death, the first of the last men on earth.

Théodora

I thought I had burned my novel, *Théodora*. I found it, unfinished and unfinishable, in my blue armoires. When *Les Nouvelles littéraires* asked me for an article on hotels, I gave them an excerpt from *Théodora*.

When T. returned, it was late. Most of the hotel's clients were asleep. He met Jean in the stairway. This meeting didn't seem to please him. Jean said good evening to T. and watched him move away, surprised all the same by his coldness. T. knew where Jean was coming from. Jean was coming from the floor above, the fifth floor of the hotel, where the governess of Bernard and Marie slept. He was returning to his own room. The rooms of Bernard and Marie and of the three other Braun children were on the fourth floor. Below them, on the third floor, were Madame Mort and Monsieur Théo, in rooms on opposite sides of the hall that stretched in front of the landing.

Jean's room was also on the third floor. The other rooms in

the hotel were occupied by couples with children. They went to bed earlier than the others—the others on these middle floors. Around these others they were spectators, whose curiosity varied with temperament, age, fatigue, degree of mutual attachment, and state of health. T. lived on the fifth floor of the hotel. This was the top floor, and on it lived Mademoiselle Koppel— temporarily, it was said, for she was supposed to change rooms come autumn.

For some time T. had been having difficulty climbing the last few flights. His heart, perhaps, or his nighttime asthma. These, at any rate, were the reasons he came up with to explain why he felt uncomfortable climbing up to his room. Some nights he thought of another reason: the staircase. It was ugly, he thought, and the maroon carpet was worn in patches. The shabbiness was apparent only at night, in the silence of the hotel, in the light that filtered in from the corridors and landings. It matched and even confouned itself with T.'s fatigue when he returned home. Then, too, the blue-gray walls were dirty, stained with children's fingerprints, and T. saw these stains more clearly at night because there were fewer people on the stairs and at that hour he walked so slowly, toward his sleep. His heart, probably. Or the war. It had just ended. There was talk of installing an elevator next year. The war. Or Théodora's love. The hotel was in Europe, in the central Alps, in a very quiet closed valley. it had been occupied by German troops. Then it was recaptured. After that it had been assigned for use by convalescent deportees. And then, two years ago, it had been returned to its owners, and the vacationers returned. T. heard the sound of his breathing in the silence of the corridor, between the rows of doors. Things were going better. Perhaps he would survive this love.

She had already returned. She was stretched out naked on the bed. That's the way it is when Théodora is sad: she undresses, she can't stand to have anything on, and she stretches out. Naked, stretched out on the bed, in the bad light of the hotel room.

"We did well not to go out. Now everything is clear," Théodora said.

Standing, it's less visible, perhaps, but when Théodora lies down, beauty reigns over her body.

"I'm hot," said Théodora softly. "It's boring in this hotel," she added.

T. sat on the edge of the bed and looked at Théodora. He caressed her leg. Théodora caused a powerful but shapeless dream to well up within him. For two years, this end, this agony, this calm.

"Maybe I'll live," said T.

"It makes no difference," Théodora said. "I'm used to you," she added.

Théodora closed her eyes as T. caressed her. His caresses became progressively more licentious. T. remained seated beside Théodora's stretched-out body. He looked at it. He touched it. He caressed it.

"I have caressed Théodora's naked body," T. wrote, "I spoke and she didn't answer me. She appeared to be asleep."

"Sometimes I still think about the war," Théodora said. "I'm used to you. I want to stay here with you in this hotel. Sometimes I think about my life, about nothing else."

I continued to caress Théodora's naked body. I said:

"We must make a change. We must separate. We must move on to other loves."

"Don't start," Théodora said.

Théodora closed her eyes as I caressed her. My caresses became progressively more licentious. I saw that as my hand moved, Théodora's sadness changed imperceptibly into slumbering thought. Probably that sadness became more and more hopeless, more and more stationary. Her entire body was immersed in it.

"I feel good," Théodora said.

I undressed quietly, without waking Théodora. I went to sleep alongside her. I took her head against my chest. Someone in the corridor passed by our door. Théodora talked in her sleep, in broken sentences and an unknown language.

Les Nouvelles littéraires, 1979

4